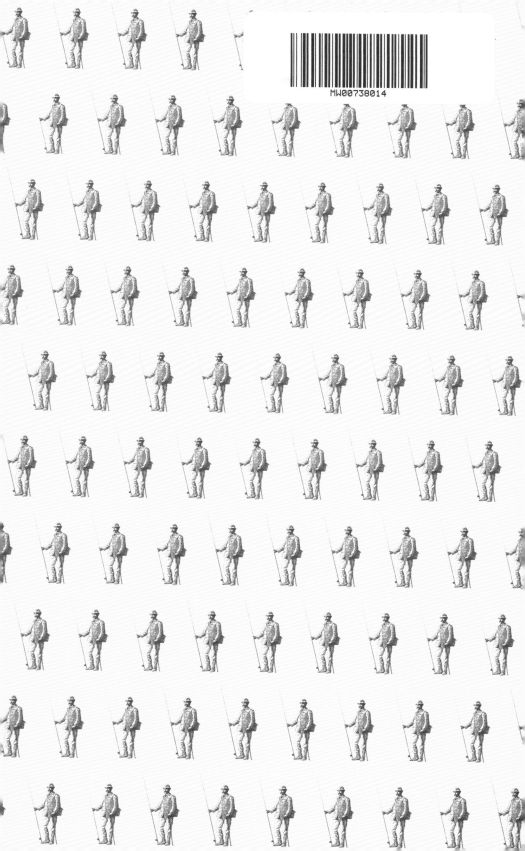

The Forgotten Flies
of Roger Woolley

Roger Woolley at his fly-tying bench

The Forgotten Flies of Roger Woolley

J N Watson

Coch-y-Bonddu Books | 2012

THE FORGOTTEN FLIES OF ROGER WOOLLEY

Written by John N Watson

First published by Coch-y-Bonddu Books, Machynlleth, 2012

Standard edition
ISBN 978 1 904784 52 4

Collector's edition
Limited to 250 signed cloth-bound copies
ISBN 978 1 904784 53 1

Flyfisher's Classic Library de luxe edition
Limited to only 30 copies
ISBN 978 1 905396 20 7

© Coch-y-Bonddu Books Ltd & John N Watson, 2012
Photography of flies by Terry Griffiths
Illustrations by Ashley Bryant

Coch-y-Bonddu Books Ltd, Machynlleth, Powys SY20 8DG
01654 702837
www.anglebooks.com

FOR EVE AND ERN

Contents

FOREWORD

Over the last 350 years there has been a school of Midland flyfishermen who have exerted considerable influence on our sport from the banks of the Dove, Manifold, Wye, Lathkill and Derwent. Theirs has been a journey of change in angling shaped by innovation and technology – from rods of hazel and blackthorn to boron wands, twisted horsehair to plastic lines and fluorocarbon.

One area where, in principal, there has been no major change is in the making of the artificial fly. Eyed hooks and a vast range of natural and synthetic materials have given greater options and convenience but the end product is still fur, feather and tinsel skilfully wrapped on a hook in an attempt to copy nature and deceive fish.

Anglers do not always have the time or inclination to create their own flies and tackle – therefore others have made their living from providing such needs. In this respect two names stand out, both from the watershed of the River Dove: in the nineteenth century, David Foster with his family business in Ashbourne, and in the twentieth century, Roger Woolley in Tutbury and Hatton.

Roger Woolley dressed flies for local anglers but such was the quality of his product that he became known to anglers worldwide. His fly-tying genius, recognised by giants of flyfishing, resulted in his ideas, methods and dressings being published in many articles and in three books. These are now out-of-print and the modern angler is in danger of losing much of Woolley's work.

John Watson and I are contemporaries, Roger Woolley was from another generation but his work was second-to-none, and was supplied from Hatton for five decades of the twentieth century, the business being taken forward a further decade after his death by one of his long-time employees, Miss Rosa Smith.

I, like John, remember climbing the stone staircase to Fosters' first floor saleroom where W L Foster, Arnold Mosley, the manager, or Gordon Hudson would supply an angler's requirements. Many of the fly patterns sold here were those of Roger Woolley. The supply of fishing tackle by mail-order had an effect on both businesses and eventually both closed in the 1970s.

This book, which results from a chance find of artefacts and notes left by Roger Woolley, gives an insight into the art of fly-tying by one of the master professionals of the last one hundred years. Here is previously unknown and unpublished material, along with details of Roger Woolley's angling life. In addition, brief sketches bring to light the names of those anglers who influenced his work.

I hope you will endeavour to tie and use some of these patterns. I particularly commend the Butcher Mayfly which has brought me many happy days of success in the month of June on the Dove, Manifold and Wye over the last fifty years.

Tight Lines!

Anthony Bridgett *2012*

ACKNOWLEDGEMENTS

This book, *The Forgotten Flies of Roger Woolley* evolved from my first, *Angling with the Fly: Flies and Anglers of Derbyshire and Staffordshire.* In the course of my research I was fortunate enough to be shown a fly book and case which had belonged to Roger Woolley, and further, to be given access to the contents along with other material. Many of the flies had not, as far as I could ascertain, been formally recorded before. Their owners accorded to me not only access, but also hospitality, heat, light and space to complete a long and involved project. If this work should be of interest and value to fly-dressers and anglers then it will be entirely due to the generous spirit in which a stranger was received.

A second collection of flies and packets was offered for study after a request for information published by *Trout & Salmon* magazine. This too was loaned in the same manner without let or hindrance.

Others have given or loaned items to me, produced supplementary research, provided introductions or endlessly tolerated my ramblings. All their contributions are greatly valued and form vital parts of the fabric herein.

My thanks and appreciation therefore go to: Peter Arfield, John Austin, Colleen and Victor Benson, Tony Bridgett, J B H Byfield, Kathleen and Bryan Chinn, Dave Clarke, Gordon Evans, Margaret and Alan Gilbert, Anne Harris, Tutbury Museum, Clive Harris, Dr. John Horner, Ray Hill, Robin Manners, Mike Nash, Keith Parsons, Terry Parker, Ken Price, Ken Smith, M A Smith, Noel Smith, Peter Toye, J S Wilton, and Steve Woolley.

The following organisations gave of their invaluable help, advice and expertise: The British Library and Reading Room Staff, Burton Mutual

AA, The Environment Agency, *Fly Fishing & Fly Tying* magazine, Staffordshire County Archives and Malinda Law (BA), *Trout & Salmon* magazine, and Tutbury Museum.

In matters practical, my thanks go to: Tim Thorpe of Derbyshire Fishing Flies who shared with me his deep knowledge and expertise, Terry Griffiths for his superb photography of Roger Woolley's flies, and Ashley Bryant for his treks to Derbyshire from Essex and his encouragement, experience and contribution of the lovely watercolour plates and vignettes.

Also to Paul Morgan of Coch-y-Bonddu Books and his colleagues, Paul Curtis and Pete MacKenzie, for their invaluable input and skills in putting the book together.

I offer my apologies to those whom I have been unable to locate or who I have inadvertently omitted to mention, and will remedy such omissions should the opportunity arise in the future.

To my wife, Anne, for her calmness in crises, endless support and complete tolerance in matters piscatorial and literary.

J N Watson *March 2012*

INTRODUCTION

Between the covers of this book the reader will find a considerable resource of previously unpublished material appertaining to the life and work of Roger Woolley, the great, yet today almost forgotten, fly-tyer and fisherman. Here are recollections from family and friends, along with information gleaned from his personal papers and letters, and thoughts and opinions from his clients, acquaintances and others. Hopefully this book will give those old enough to remember him fresh insights into a remarkable man and will also introduce Roger Woolley to those unfamiliar with his knowledge, craftsmanship and watercraft.

My own introduction was one wet October afternoon in 1961 when I was in Foster Bros, Church Street, Ashbourne buying some cartridges. It was whilst browsing round the upstairs showroom waiting to be served that I first heard the name 'Roger Woolley' or more properly, overheard it. Another customer, who was buying flies, was being assisted by the manager (who, I now realise, was probably Mr Arnold Mosley) when one of them said 'Roger Woolley's Steel Blue is a popular grayling fly'. The two gentlemen were selecting patterns from a drawer and Woolley's name cropped up regularly throughout the conversation.

At the time my interests lay more with the gun and carp rod than with a split cane wand and 'upstream dry'. Even so, this earnest discussion interested me sufficiently to tentatively enquire about grayling flies and fishing when my time came to be served. The detailed information given was stored for future reference – the meagre wage of a farm student-cum-labourer did not lend itself to such activities, however fascinating they may have appeared. At this time I was a regular, if secretive, visitor to Bradbourne and Bentley brooks, but only the odd small trout was lured by the delicately presented worm – no grayling. If truth be told, worm seemed a far superior bait to fur and feather at that time.

Years later, the fly rod was adopted and with it the desire to dress flies rather than purchase them. In any case, that wonderful upstairs showroom had disappeared! The process of fly-tying was slow but sure, and after many visits to the waterside a few trout began to approve of the offerings gleaned from books and magazines. The acknowledgement 'Woolley' followed the names of some patterns and I was surprised to learn he had spent most of his life in Hatton and Tutbury, quite close to my own home near Derby.

More recently, whilst involved with research for another book, *Angling with the Fly*, I was introduced to relatives of Roger Woolley. They had inherited a large collection of material about his life, his fly-dressing business, and his highly-regarded ability as an angler. The collection comprised several hundred flies, many of which probably had never been recorded, together with photographs, sketches, articles and personal papers. I felt it was important that this new material was brought to light to the fishing public, and that it would be a shame if it was left to slip into obscurity. I also believed that it was perhaps important to bring renewed focus on a man who was an expert angler and fly-dresser on the River Dove and an important figure in the angling heritage of this country.

Woolley was a fly-dresser and angler of influence locally and nationally, but his name and achievements have largely been forgotten except as a postscript to fly dressings in tying manuals and angling bibliographies. Although amongst fishers on the Dove and Derwent watersheds his memory still lingers on and his patterns, as always, still take their toll.

Recognising his skill and innovative fly-dressing, RB Marston, editor of the *Fishing Gazette*, invited Roger to write a series of articles for the magazine. These were well received and republished in two books, *Modern Trout Fly Dressing* (1932) and *The Flyfisher's Flies* (1938). In June 1933 the following reference to Roger appeared in the *Fishing Gazette*, presumably written by Marston: 'There is no need to enlarge on the reputation of the author as a Fly Tyer. He is one of the best Fly Tyers in the trade and his flies have probably been used on most trout and grayling waters at home and abroad.'

Roger was at the forefront of what was then modern fly-dressing, and during his lifetime was well-known to other angling 'celebrities'. He was perhaps best known as a grayling angler – long before the species reached its present popularity. William Carter Platts asked for his opinion when writing *Grayling Fishing* (1939) and the flyfishing surgeon, Richard Lake, asked him to write chapters on fly and bait fishing for his book *The Grayling* (1942). GEM Skues lauded Woolley's skill as an entomologist and fly-dresser. The comprehensive catalogues produced by Woolley listed the patterns of Halford, Tod, Skues, Edmonds and Lee, Dunne, and Bridgett – presumably with their permission.

With these considerations in mind I spent many months collating information and analysing the 'new' previously undiscovered or unrecorded patterns and material and combining it with previously published knowledge about Woolley and his flies. The process has certainly enhanced and improved my own fly-dressing and angling abilities. Researching and writing this book has also given me a great deal of pleasure – hopefully *The Forgotten Flies of Roger Woolley* will bring Roger's life and work to the attention of 21st century anglers and in some small way give the same pleasure to its readers.

HOW TO USE THIS BOOK

A few words regarding the use of *The Forgotten Flies of Roger Woolley* may be helpful. The book is intended as a resource for fly-dressers and, as such, several of the chapters and appendices are separate entities. I have found it enjoyable to experiment with various aspects of Woolley's work – fly-dressing, use of materials he recommended and some of his angling methods; perhaps others will too.

Chapter Two highlights groups of flies enabling the fly-dresser to locate fly styles of interest. Each fly is numbered within its group and listed under a heading, so:

Group: General Flies and Fancy Wet Flies
Style: Grouse Wing Series. Nos., 1 – 8

The principal groups include Hackled Flies, Bumbles, Aphids, Midges and Gnats, General and Fancy Wet Flies, Fan Winged Mayflies, Hacklepoint Mayflies, Butcher Mayflies, Loch Wet Flies, Salmon and Sea-trout Flies and Low Water Style Flies. Details of relevant plates appertaining to the groups are also included.

For those wishing to experiment with 'new' or 'forgotten' patterns and dressing materials and methods there is considerable scope here. It might be of interest, for example, to select Roger Woolley named or unnamed patterns similar in style to standard or modern patterns normally used and see how they perform.

Details are given of the fly-dressing materials favoured by Woolley – some are unobtainable or very difficult to source today but others have simply been forgotten or superseded by the multiplicity of modern products. It is a pleasant process to tie flies with natural and unfamiliar materials and to find the results work just as well as those of today.

By 21st century standards Woolley's fly-dressing tools were rudimentary, but he possessed great skill. He held the hook in his fingers – a mounted needle, scissors, wax and varnish being the other necessities. With a little practice simple flies, flies which catch fish, can be tied on the riverbank. A reel of silk and a few hackles take up little space in the pocket. The process was good enough for Cotton, Turton, Woolley… today it may seem a little contrived, but if the exercise adds to the enjoyment of fly-tying and fishing, why not? Many of the flies listed are suitable for the process of tying 'in the hand.'

There is now considerable interest in using vintage tackle, or modern copies thereof, and anglers may well be interested in tying up and experimenting with the original dressings featured in this book, all of which are ideal for use with 'retro' tackle and tactics. Woolley recommended several personal angling methods – one example was fishing downstream for grayling. No doubt this will be considered heresy by some, but it is worth a try where conscience and regulations allow.

Walton, Cotton, Venables, Chetham, Blacker, Fitzgibbon, Ogden, Foster, Halford, Skues, Marryat, Marston – the roll call of famous anglers is long. Included here are those who are less well-known – except around their own rivers and localities. People Roger Woolley fished with and called friends. They are not all familiar names but they have all made their contribution to flyfishing, sometimes only in the form of a single named pattern. How many anglers who have fished the Derbyshire and Staffordshire streams for grayling would be without a Double Badger? How many have tried Oakden's Claret or Tommy's Favourite for trout? Woolley tied up these patterns for those he knew but he was not the originator of them. His books and catalogues reveal other unfamiliar names – a rich resource for anyone interested in flies, fly-tying and angling.

And it is as such a resource I hope this book will be most used. It is not designed for the coffee table or dusty bookcase – but will be most at home on a corner of the fly-dressing table, well-thumbed with numerous book-marks and varnish stains.

Roger Woolley's Steel Blue

Chapter One

Roger Woolley's Early Life and Career

Personally I always start my day's grayling fishing with two fancy flies, fished wet, invariably the Grayling Witch and the Grayling Steel Blue
                                                    — The Grayling

Thomas Roger Woolley was born at Tutbury, Staffordshire in January 1877, into a typically large Victorian family. The family home was in Burton Street. The fifth child of his parents, he had five brothers and three sisters. In his formative years he was fascinated by water, aquatic insects and other riverside flora and fauna, evidently encouraged in these interests by his siblings or parents. There was no shortage of water around Tutbury and generations of children must have peered over the stone parapets of Tutbury Bridge into the River Dove beneath. Here Roger may have seen barbel or grayling shoaling over the gravel bed; almost certainly he would have dipped a home-made net into those clear waters and emptied his catch into a jar or dish to observe the contents. There were several ponds and a mill-stream nearby too; lots of opportunities for an aspiring naturalist to extend his observations and studies.

Roger fished from an early age, probably in the company of his father, John, a glassmaker by trade who in his leisure time was reputed to be a good shot as well as an angler. These initial expeditions would most likely be in pursuit of coarse fish since Roger's involvement with flyfishing seems to have developed during his teens. This appears to be contradicted by an interview in an article (seen as an undated newspaper or magazine cutting of unknown source) entitled *Give Me a Witch and a Steel Blue*. When the author, Hilda Brown, asked Woolley, by then over eighty years old, how he began fly-dressing he replied as follows:

'Well, when I was a little lad – that'll be over seventy years ago you know – I wanted to go fishing but the flies cost two pence each,

Burton Street, Tutbury – Roger Woolley was born in one of the gabled houses beyond the van.

Tutbury Endowed Boys' School where Roger was a pupil

and two pence was a lot in those days. So I set to and made my own flies.'

Years of observing insects and fish certainly formed a substantial foundation for his fly-dressing methods. He always sought to imitate the natural insect with his dressings, except fancy flies for grayling, sea-trout and salmon which he referred to as 'just imagination.' Insects caught at the waterside were transported home and every attempt made to copy them with such materials as were to hand. He is believed to have kept records and observations in note-books, also eagerly devouring the information contained in books and magazines.

Roger Woolley left school when he was thirteen or fourteen years old – not unusual for a working-class child in the late nineteenth century. Despite what he described as 'little schooling' he was a particularly determined individual and worked hard at those things he enjoyed and which interested him. His expertise in entomology came from years of practical experience and personal research by the waterside. Many good naturalists owe much of their ability and knowledge to informal childhood and teenage years of watching, observing and experimenting. These activities aside, there would have been the necessity to earn a living (Victorian attitudes and parents were not necessarily too keen on the concept of gap-years), and Roger obtained work on a farm or the local estate as a groom, learning to work with horses and vehicles.

He then took what would seem to be a somewhat brave and adventurous step for a young man from the Midlands of England. In 1896, at the age of nineteen, he obtained the post of coachman on an Irish estate. It is very unlikely that he would have been appointed to such a position without good previous experience and references – by that age young men would have been expected to have years of training and work experience behind them.

The estate was that of the Chetwynd family; it would seem likely that they were related to the Chetwynds of Ingestre near Stafford, which is no great distance from Woolley's home in Tutbury. There are two possible locations for the estate, one in County Fermanagh, the other in County Kerry. Of the former the only reference I have is in the manuscripts of

The Woolley family in the early 1900s
Back row: Wilfred, Jack, Harry, Fred, Roger
Front row: Lizzie, John and Elizabeth (parents), Sarah

Roger Woolley's son-in-law, a local Tutbury historian, which refers to Roger being 'in gentleman's service' with the Chetwynds. The County Kerry estate was the seat of Richard Walter Chetwynd, seventh Viscount of Bearhaven who died in 1911. There may have been a property in the north but further detail is lacking.

The somewhat enclosed community of a large estate, coupled with long hours of work or service, meant that the employees spent much of their time in each other's company. Strong friendships were made as, I am sure, were enmities. Roger Woolley became acquainted with a riverkeeper or gamekeeper on the estate who was a good angler and fly-dresser. Roger evidently got on with this older man, his own experience and knowledge acquired on the banks of the Dove enabling him to discuss matters piscatorial. The keeper was prepared to spend time teaching the new recruit to fish and dress flies. A coachman's hours would be long and erratic but it is not difficult to imagine the master and apprentice using available time, on long summer evenings and wild winter nights, to fish, dress flies or simply discuss angling. Roger's progress pleased his teacher, who had found an eager and demanding pupil well capable of absorbing all the skills and information offered by his mentor. Further opportunities to develop these new skills were available in the local rivers and loughs containing runs of salmon and sea-trout. Simply by watching others fish much could be learned by an interested young man. As a friend of the keeper, Roger was probably given the chance to fish these waters from time to time and was taught to dress suitable patterns to use on these occasions. Years later, writing in *Modern Trout Fly Dressing*, Roger Woolley included a fly with the imaginative (or not so imaginative) name of an 'Irish Pattern'. Was this his mentor's favourite pattern, a souvenir of his time in Ireland, or simply a coincidence?

Another meeting, and one of even greater significance, took place during his stay in Ireland. Roger met a young lady, also in the employ of the Chetwynd estate. Her name was Minnie Truman, and she would become Mrs Roger Woolley. Minnie's family had Irish roots, her grandmother being born in Killeshandra, County Cavan.

In 1898, after two years in Ireland, Roger and Minnie returned to Tutbury and in January 1901 they were married at Gnosall. The 1901 census shows Roger as a railway wagon repairer living in Tutbury. During this period he set up in business as a barber and hairdresser, skills he may have acquired in Ireland. He was a sociable man, as are many barbers, with a good sense of humour; both characteristics important in dealing with clients at a personal level. At times he was capable of playing the odd practical joke with his razor in hand – how well that went down is open to question. He was considered to be quite a character!

Some time later Roger and Minnie moved to Marston Road just across the River Dove to Hatton in Derbyshire. Word of Roger's skill, both as an angler and fly-dresser, rapidly spread throughout the locality. He regularly fished the local rivers, often at the invitation of friends or clients. On these expeditions fly-dressings inevitably changed hands and those tied by Roger were very successful, gaining a well-deserved reputation. Before long he began to get enquiries for flies and was asked to tie and supply them for local anglers, alongside his hairdressing business and now part time insurance agency! Anglers requiring flies visited the barber's shop and gave their order. If the flies were not available, hooks and materials were put up in an envelope and sent to other premises across the road with pattern details for his fly-dressers. For many years his daughters assisted him in tying flies, but as time passed and business expanded other helpers were employed. Prepared flies and materials were kept in a back room behind the barber shop. Since Roger was a very sociable person, during slack times in his barber's shop he was happy to talk angling and fly-dressing with customers. Possibly disadvantaging himself, he introduced to others the skills required to produce their own flies.

In the early years of the twentieth century he became an official of Tutbury Congregational Church. His commitment to this organisation was lifelong and he held several offices within it; beginning as a member of the choir, he became a Sunday school teacher, later its Superintendent, ultimately a church trustee, and served as Deacon for around forty years and Life Deacon for ten.

Throughout the years leading up to the First World War the hairdressing fly-tyer built up his clientele. Like millions of others, the lives of the Woolleys were rudely interrupted by hostilities. Roger joined the Royal Army Medical Corps and found himself in Egypt, 'soldiering', as he put it.

During the years, while he was away, Minnie carried on with all his business interests, along with bringing up the family. They had four daughters, at this time all in various stages of training as fly-dressers, assisting their mother with the completion of orders and in running the business. Of the letters Roger sent home during his war service, some were specifically written for his children, recounting some of his experiences, enquiring how the fly-dressing was progressing, and encouraging them to support their mother in every possible way.

The house on Marston Road, the site of Roger Woolley's home and business as barber and fly-dresser.

After his return from the war Roger was able to settle back into Hatton and such normality as the war had left behind, to continue with his life. It was around this time he was appointed to the office of Church Deacon.

In the 1920s he produced catalogues for his fly-dressing business, *A List of Special Trout and Grayling Flies*. Running to 40 pages, these were not only lists of flies for sale, but also a distillation of much experience, anecdote and advice for angling clients. Whether or not these were

Roger's first efforts at angling literature cannot be established, but they convey much that is of value to anglers even 90 years later, such is their content and detail. Furthermore, they are written in concise and lively prose while, of course, extolling the product they advertise.

In the late 1920s and early 1930s, he wrote a series of articles for the *Fishing Gazette*, then under the editorship of R B Marston. His articles must have been very well received by the angling public as in 1932 they formed the basis for his first book, *Modern Trout Fly Dressing*. This volume ran to two further editions in his lifetime and was considered a standard work on its subject. Most available copies have been very well thumbed! Catalogues continued to appear over ensuing years, the format remaining much the same, but keeping up with new developments in angling, fly-dressing and fly patterns. A feature of some later editions are humorous cartoons which serve to laud Roger Woolley's fly patterns and also included at this time were black and white photographs of special styles of fly.

A further series of articles written in the late 1930s resulted, by public demand, in a second book by Woolley. *The Fly-Fisher's Flies*, published by the *Fishing Gazette* in 1938, was a concise volume detailing a lifetime's observation of natural flies of interest to trout and anglers. This, too, was destined to run for a further two editions.

By now Roger Woolley was a highly respected professional fly-dresser whose work was known for both quality and innovation. Although Roger had trained his four daughters to dress flies and to assist him at busy times, the weight of business became such that he took on long-term employees. It took three months to teach each trainee to tie to the required standard. Speed was an important factor and so it took time to become really proficient. Roger dealt with orders, requisitions and clients, but still dressed flies and, as always, he inspected all the work, making sure that the quality of the final product was up to standard. While not a hard businessman, he was said to have a rather severe attitude in the workroom.

Three fly-dressers who worked for him had a combined length service of 58 years, so perhaps Roger's bark was worse than his bite. One of these ladies, Miss Rosa Smith, bought the business after Roger Woolley died, and continued running it for many years from premises in Bridge Street, Tutbury.

His reputation as a grayling angler spread far beyond the confines of the River Dove. For his book, *Grayling Fishing* (1939), W Carter Platts asked for Roger's advice on the presentation of the dry fly to grayling and his recommendations for suitable fly patterns. G E M Skues praised Roger's entomological and fly-dressing skills in his book, *Nymph Fishing for Chalk Stream Trout*. In 1943 Richard Lake invited Woolley to contribute chapters on bait and flyfishing to the second, expanded edition of his book *The Grayling*, first published a year earlier. By this time Roger was in his late sixties, but still active and interested in angling and fly-dressing. The entry *Woolley, Roger,* was to be found in the indexes of many angling tomes, as it still is today.

In 1948 Roger formed a limited company: Roger Woolley & Co. Ltd., with his four daughters as directors and himself as managing director. Minnie Woolley died in 1949 but he continued working until shortly before his death in November 1959.

Roger Woolley's flybook and fly-case

CHAPTER TWO

The 'Forgotten' Flies

. . . those pretty coloured concoctions that are the result of imagination only — The Grayling

The fly-dressings listed in this chapter are, in the main, taken from Roger Woolley's surviving fly book and fly-case, both of which have been preserved by one of his close relatives. A few further flies were contained in 'Roger Woolley' printed envelopes used to send flies to various clients which were shown to me by other collectors. I have appended notes to these flies when listed.

Only a handful of the patterns in the books are actually named by Roger, these having handwritten labels; the substantial remainder being unlabelled. Most of the unlabelled material (and the labelled ones for that matter) are, as far as it has been possible to establish, original patterns not previously listed or described.

Those contained in the 'Roger Woolley' fly envelopes are annotated with the name of the pattern or patterns concerned. These flies may not have been dressed by Woolley's hand, but by one of his fly-dressers. If this was the case they would have been subject to stringent scrutiny by Woolley before dispatched to customers. There are also a number of what appear to be recognisable 'standard' patterns present. These I have named, although some of the names are open to opinion! A basic index is provided to give easier access to the styles and groups of the unnamed dressings.

Also included in this chapter are some dressings taken directly from Woolley's first book, *Modern Trout Fly Dressing* which was published in 1932 by the *Fishing Gazette*.

Other flyfishing and fly-tying historians may find it of interest to know exactly how I analysed and catalogued the fly-book and fly-case, and the other material. It took time and patience and some experience and intuition, but was always a fascinating project. What follows is my basic methodology:

The 'fly book' consists of four felt leaves interspersed with vellum. These are bound in what appears to be an old black hard-back notebook, the front of which is now missing. The leaves are hand-sewn through the spine. The case measures seven by four-and-a-half inches and is three-quarters of an inch thick. Moths have damaged the felt considerably and flies at the leaf edges have also suffered. Flies are caught in on both sides of the felt leaves, and there was also a tangle of flies to horsehair and gut, loose between two pages. This has now been teased out and the flies from it packed in plastic envelopes. A large salmon iron was also loose in the case.

The flies in this case are roughly grouped according to style: large loch-style patterns, perhaps suitable for both brown and sea-trout; wet flies of a number of series such as Heckhams, Grouse and Teal; sea-trout and salmon flies, and a range of mayfly styles mixed with duns, hackles, bumbles and fancy flies. Apart from the smallest patterns there are very few dry flies.

The 'fly-case' is a black japanned tin measuring two-and-a-half by one-and-three-quarter inches. It has obviously had a good deal of use and the inside of the lid bears the legend, 'Roger Woolley, Tutbury'. The box is lined with a piece of coarse, stiff material in which the flies are caught. The flies in this case are, in the main, very small patterns of aphids, midges and duns, all dressed on tiny eyed hooks, some as small as sizes 22 or 24.

There are flies tied to hair or gut, gut-eyed patterns and various styles of eyed hooks. Many of those tied to gut have probably been kept as reference patterns, as the gut or hair has perished and broken off close to the fly head and they are no longer suitable for fishing. Others have never been used, still in coils of three as they were put up after tying was completed. Hooks vary in type according to the pattern of fly, some blued, others japanned or bronzed. There are sneck bends, round bends and sproat bends. Many of the flies could be used just as they are, decades after Roger Woolley stored them away.

The flies were somewhat mixed and many unrecognisable, so I needed to devise a system of recording. In order to disturb the flies as little as possible, the leaves of the fly-case were photographed and each fly numbered in Indian ink, giving a position to each fly which could be compared to those in the case. From these photographs a basic analysis of each pattern was recorded, noting a query wherever materials, colours or sizes were in doubt. I didn't want to remove the flies from the owners' home so these reference photographs enabled the recording to proceed elsewhere at leisure, to be checked with the originals later. This process was successful, giving a good framework on which to complete the recording from the actual dressings.

A hook gauge from the frontispiece of Roger Woolley's *Modern Trout Fly Dressing* was used to assess the size of hooks; other aids were forceps to handle the flies and a dissecting needle to probe the structure and materials used in each dressing. Magnification was provided by a two inch diameter 5x lens and the flies viewed in natural daylight.

Making the final analysis of the flies proved to be rather more arduous than anticipated: sessions had to be limited to two or three hours since after this time accuracy rapidly diminished. A tape recorder was employed for the first session but proved unsuccessful. Subsequently, each fly was examined and the dressing described in a different colour on the master sheets created from the photographs. A fair copy of the dressings was then made and notes relating to further queries listed, to be resolved at the next visit. This took a number of sessions but resulted in accurate descriptions of the collection. The collection contained 311 flies.

In addition, included as Appendix Five, are a further 141 flies, named and unnamed, from other sources. These, while associated with Roger Woolley and dressed in his style, have no absolute provenance as such; some are in Roger Woolley packets but could have been dressed by his daughters or his fly-dressers. Nevertheless they are of sufficient interest to warrant recording.

Where present the following features were examined:

ACTUAL SIZES OF HOOKS USED THROUGHOUT THIS BOOK

New Nos.		Old Nos.
000		17
00		16
0		15
1		14
2		13
3		12
4		11
5		10
6		9
7		8
8		7
9		6
10		5

Hook guide from Modern Trout Fly Dressing by Roger Woolley used to assess hook sizes. (Actual size)

Hook size: style, number and finish

e.g. 5 ls x 2 eyed = New Size 5 - 2 eyed hooks

Means of attachment: tied direct to gut, gut-eyed or eyed

Whisks or tail, tag, tip, butt: materials where applicable

Body materials and rib details

Hackle, wing and head

Where other details are pertinent they are included with the dressing. Some of the flies are standard patterns; others are Roger Woolley's own dressings already listed in his writings and where this is the case the names are included with the dressing. Caution has been used in this process and where doubt exists no title has been appended. The patterns have been detailed as a simple historical record but it is almost inevitable there are dressings in the lists which have not been recognised. However, unnamed dressings have not been previously listed, as far as can be determined.

The dressing descriptions are as accurate as possible, despite several difficulties which emerged; moth damage was surprisingly comprehensive where it occurred. Larvae are extremely efficient at completely removing whisks, hackles and even wings in such a manner as to make it practically impossible to find evidence of materials being present. One fly was so altered that at first I recorded it as a 'buzzer.' Later I found its twin which had more obvious remains of hackle and wings.

Tinsels are subject to corrosion and tarnishing. The former destroys the surface making it awkward to see whether gold or silver tinsel has been used. Tarnishing gives more interesting results. A variety of colours are produced, some very attractive. One fly in particular has a red lurex-like tip which I believe to be flat silver tinsel but I am not certain. It is easy to confuse tarnished silver wire with black thread, particularly if the wire is fine.

Practically all the furs and feathers used in fly-dressing can be subject to fading, or discolouration such as foxing, or stains from hooks and other materials. This makes accurate identification of similar feathers very difficult. Good daylight is helpful, but sometimes an educated guess, with the appropriate qualification, is the last resort. Ageing does seem to affect some materials more than others; wings made from fibres of speckled turkey or bronze mallard can be very awkward to differentiate.

The flies contained in the cases are a snapshot of some patterns created and tied by Roger Woolley, ranging from tiny midges to a huge salmon fly and a selection of older mayfly patterns. There are few dry flies, no nymphs, and despite his later enthusiasm for hackle-fibre winged patterns, no examples of those either. These two fly-cases would only have been a small part of Woolley's collection. The date of the cases and their contents is unknown but many of the dressing styles and attachments appear to have been made earlier rather than later in his career. They may have been personal favourites, good sellers or successful patterns retained for certain clients – we will never know.

A leaf from Roger Woolley's flybook

Hackle Flies

This selection of patterns is of simple flies – a number dressed on small hooks and reminiscent of the Northern or Midland spiders or Rough Water Devon style patterns. The former are dressed with soft mobile hen or game bird hackles, the latter with cock hackles. The larger patterns in this section may be suitable as loch, lake or sea-trout flies but as hackled patterns they are appended here.

1. *Hook* :   000 to gut, sneck
    Body :   Peacock herl, ribbed 3 turns fine gold oval
    Hackle :   Hook length, bright red cock, 2 turns

2. *Hook* :   000 to gut
    Body :   Very dark peacock herl
    Hackle :   Red cock

3. *Hook* :   000 sneck down-eyed
    Tail :   Fine yellow wool or floss silk
    Body :   White silk ribbed with peacock herl
    Hackle: Buff hen

4. *Hook* :   00 ls x 2 down-eyed
    Whisks :   Buff feather fibres
    Body :   Green peacock herl
    Hackle :   Light blue dun hen

5. Red Tag
    Hook :   00 eyed
    Tag :   Bright red floss silk
    Tip :   Flat silver tinsel
    Body :   Peacock herl
    Hackle :   Medium red cock

6.   *Hook* :   0 or 1 eyed
   Tag :   Red wool
   Body :   Bronze peacock herl
   Hackle :   Sparse, brown hen, 2 turns
   Head Tag :   Red wool
   (Apart from the wing-colour this fly is as Bradshaw's Fancy.)

7.   *Hook* :   0 eyed, sneck
   Silk :   Yellow
   Body :   Dun feather fibre
   Hackle :   Grouse covert

8.   *Hook* :   1 eyed
   Silk :   Black
   Body :   Plump hare's ear fur, ribbed 3 turns hackle stalk
   Hackle :   Dark dun cock 3 turns, thick and long

9.   Blue Dun
   Hook :   1 eyed
   Whisks :   3 dun cock hackle fibres
   Body :   Ash seal's fur, ribbed 4 turns primrose silk
   Hackle :   Dun cock, 2 turns

10.   March Brown
   Hook :   2 down-eyed
   Whisks :   Speckled partridge fibres
   Body :   Dubbed hare's ear fur, ribbed 4 turns gold wire
   Hackle :   Speckled brown partridge

11.   *Hook* :   2 down-eyed
   Tail :   White wool
   Body :   Bronze peacock herl, ribbed 3 turns flat silver tinsel
   Hackle :   Red cock

12.   *Hook* :   6 to gut, japanned
      Whisks :   Light red cock hackle
      Body :   Oval gold tinsel, 12
      Hackle :   Light red cock, bushy

13.   *Hook* :   7 to gut, japanned
      Tip :   Oval silver tinsel
      Whisks :   Feather fibre, stained red or possibly Ibis fibre
      Body :   Chrome yellow seal's fur, ribbed 4 turns double oval silver
                    tinsel
      Hackle :   Blue dun cock, long and bushy

14.   *Hook* :   7 to gut, japanned
      Whisks :   Brown feather fibre
      Body :   Orange seal's fur, ribbed 4 turns oval gold tinsel
      Hackle :   Dark speckled hen pheasant covert or breast

15.   *Hook* :   8 to gut, japanned
      Hackle :   Several light red or ginger
                    cock, wound one after
                    another from the bend to
                    shoulder

(The final hackle is lighter in shade, the whole being similar to a Loch Ordie except in colour. The hackles are long and densely packed).

19

16. *Hook* : 8 gut-eyed, japanned
    Tip : Flat gold tinsel
    Tail : Scarlet wool
    Body : Black seal's fur, ribbed 3
    or 4 turns flat gold tinsel
    Hackle : Black hen, full and
    bushy
    Head : Black varnish

17. *Hook* : 5 down-eyed, bronzed
    Tail : Sparse red feather fibre
    Body : Claret seal's fur, ribbed 5
    turns fine oval gold tinsel
    Hackle : Long red cock, long
    speckled turkey or
    similar, in front

18. *Hook* : 7 down-eyed, possibly x 2
    long, japanned
    Tail : Red feather fibre
    Body : 2 in Worm Fly style,
    green peacock herl each
    ribbed with 5 turns fine
    oval gold tinsel
    Hackles : Light red hen, one
    amidships, one at head

19. *Hook* :   9 to gut, japanned
    Body :   Cardinal red seal's fur, ribbed 6 turns medium flat silver tinsel
    Hackle :   Cock stained cardinal red, very full
    Head :   Black varnish

20. *Hook* :   9 to gut, japanned
    Body :   Red wool, palmered with light red cock hackle, ribbed 4 turns
                   flat gold tinsel
    Hackle :   Black hen, probably two or three hackles used, extending down
                   one third of the body

21. *Hook* :   10 down-eyed, possibly x 2 long,
                   bronzed
    Tail :   Bright orange floss silk, full
    Body :   Orange dubbing, possibly
                   chopped seal's fur seal's fur,
                   palmered badger cock hackle, 4
                   turns
    Hackle :   Badger cock, long and bushy, two
                   or three hackles

'Utility' Patterns

Listed in some catalogues, these have sparse dressings and long hackles.

1. *Hook* :   1 x 2 long, down-eyed,
                   bronzed
    Whisks :   Dark dun cock
    Body :   Purple silk
    Hackle :   Two, long and sparse.
                   Stained orange cock;
                   black cock

2. *Hook* :   1 x 2 long, down-eyed, bronzed
    Whisks :   Grizzle cock
    Body :   Light olive silk, ribbed 4 turns gold wire
    Thorax :   Ball of light olive and pale brown seal's fur mix
    Hackle :   Long, sparse badger cock

Bumbles and Bustards

Bumbles

Bumbles are old Derbyshire fly patterns which may have evolved from the Palmers of Izaak Walton, Charles Cotton and earlier anglers. David Foster of Ashbourne was probably the first to formally record the patterns but almost certainly the dressings had been passed on by word of mouth or handwritten manuscripts long before Foster's time. They were used to good effect from the 1860s by three generations of the Eatons from Matlock. All were christened George James, and as tackle makers and guides they promoted the flies to their clients.

Roger Woolley thought a great deal of Bumble patterns and used them regularly, particularly for grayling fishing. Some of his patterns were modified from those of Foster, but he was also the originator of new patterns. Some he 'padded with lead' and tied on small doubles for winter grayling fishing in order to sink quickly and deep for the larger fish. Woolley always began his angling day with a Steel Blue on his cast, and whilst not called 'bumble' the dressing is total Bumble style.

Bumbles incorporate peacock herl, floss silks and palmered hackles in their construction, can be fished wet or dry, and are usually dressed on hook sizes 0 – 2 Old Scale.

Modern Trout Fly Dressing lists Mulberry, Honey Dun, Rough, Light, Ruby and Yellow Bumbles. The following were in his personal fly book:

1.   Ruby Bumble
       Hook :   1 eyed
       Silk :   Brown
       Tip :   Ruby floss
       Body :   Ruby floss, ribbed blue-green peacock herl
       Hackle :   Shoulder to tail, pale blue dun cock, ribbed with silver wire

2.   Honey Dun Bumble
       Hook :   00 to gut, sneck, blued
       Body :   Straw floss, may be faded primrose, ribbed with 5 turns green peacock herl and claret silk, palmered honey dun cock, shoulder to tail

3.   Light Bumble Variant
       Hook :   00 to gut, sneck
       Body :   Orange and claret floss, ribbed 4 turns green peacock herl, palmered pale blue dun cock tail to shoulder

4.   *Hook* :   00 to gut, sneck
       Silk :   Red
       Body :   White floss, ribbed 4 turns green peacock sword, palmered blue dun hen hackle
       Shoulder hackle :   Ginger hen

5. *Hook* :   00 to gut, sneck
     Body :   Straw or white floss silk, ribbed 4 turns bronze peacock herl
     Hackle :   Palmered pale blue dun or faded honey dun hen

6.   *Hook* :   000 to gut
         Body :   White floss, ribbed 4 turns green peacock sword over the hackle
         Hackle :   Honey dun or ginger hen, dressed from part way up the body to the head in 'Stewart Spider' style

7.   *Hook* :   0 or 1 eyed
         Tip :   Red silk
         Body :   Peacock herl
         Hackle :   Palmered black cock

8.   Red Palmer
         Hook :   0 or 1 eyed
         Body :   Green peacock herl
         Hackle :   Palmered red cock tail to shoulder
         (In Roger Woolley fly packet as 'Steel Blue').

9.   Steel Blue
         Hook :   2 down-eyed bronzed
         Body :   Peacock herl, ribbed gold wire, with three turns of orange silk at tail end
         Hackle :   Grizzled blue cock, from shoulder to tail. The hackle fibres are long and wound quite thickly

Bustards

1.   *Hook* :   7 to gut, japanned
         Body :   Cream lamb's wool, palmered ginger hackle, ribbed 5 turns oval gold tinsel
         Hackle :   Ginger cock
         Wing :   Upright, smoky grey mallard wing quill

2. *Hook* :   9 to gut japanned
    Tip :   Light brown floss silk
    Body :   White floss silk, palmered 4 turns badger cock hackle
    Hackle :   Pale blue dun cock
    Wing :   Two pairs, white satin duck feather fibre
    Head :   Peacock herl

These may well be sedge dressings, but are in Bustard style. The origins of both are ultimately 'stick or cad baits'.

Aphids, Midges and Gnats

These flies are in a separate small black japanned tin case. Some of the patterns are duplicated, others not. All are dressed on tiny hooks and in the absence of a suitable hook gauge they are sized as the Old Redditch Hook Scale. Woolley notes in his contribution to Richard Lake's book, *The Grayling*, 'The artificial midge must be tied very small to be effective, on a hook about half the size of a 000.'

He advises that midges be dressed with 'fore and aft' hackles in some of his writings but few of those in the fly-case are tied up in this way.

The lid of the case bears the inscription 'Roger Woolley, Tutbury', in red paint.

1. *Hook* :   20 or 22 eyed
    Body :   Green seal's fur
    Hackle :   Pale blue dun cock

2. Green Aphid
    Hook :   20 or 22 eyed
    Body :   Bulky, yellow-green
                 dubbing
    Hackle :   Pale blue dun cock
                 tied amidships

3. Green Insect
    Hook :   20 or 22
    Body :   Green peacock herl
    Hackle :   Cream cock

(The three dressings above may be Woolley's variants of the Green Insect, a pattern much used on Derbyshire and Staffordshire streams for grayling.)

4. *Hook* :   20 or 22 eyed
    Body :   Cream feather fibre
    Hackle :   White or pale blue dun cock, 2 turns

5. *Hook* :   18 up-eyed
    Whisks :   Light red cock
                 hackle fibres
    Body :   Stripped quill
    Hackle :   Light red cock
    Wing :   Brown feather,
                 blackbird or thrush
                 quill

6. Black Midge
    Hook :   18 eyed
    Body :   Sparse, black silk
    Hackle :   Black cock

7.   *Hook* :   18 or 20 eyed
      Body :   Buff feather fibre
      Hackle :   Black cock

8.   *Hook* :   20 eyed
      Body :   White feather fibre, ribbed yellow and red silk
      Hackle :   Pale blue dun or white cock

9.   *Hook* :   20 or 22 down-eyed
      Body :   Pinkish quill with herl
      Hackle :   Black hen

10.   *Hook* :   20 or 22 eyed
      Body :   Peacock herl
      Hackle :   Black hen

11.   *Hook* :   20 eyed
      Body :   Bulky, peacock herl
      Hackle :   Bright red cock

12.   *Hook* :   20 or 22 down-eyed
      Body :   Sparse, black silk
      Hackle :   Cream or pale blue dun
                     cock

13.   Black Gnat
      Hook :   18 eyed
      Body :   Black silk
      Hackle :   Black cock
      Wing :   White feather quill

14. *Hook* : 20 eyed
    Body : Peacock herl
    Hackle : Black hen or cock
    Wing : Small, white feather quill

15. *Hook* : 20 eyed
    Body : Bulky, bronze peacock herl
    Hackle : White cock

16. *Hook* : 18 eyed
    Whisks : Long, Greenwell cock hackle fibres
    Body : Red silk
    Hackle : Light dun cock

17. *Hook* : 18 eyed
    Body : Cream dubbing, ribbed 3 to 4 turns primrose silk
    Hackle : Light red or pale blue dun cock

18. *Hook* : 20 eyed
    Body : Dark brown feather fibre
    Hackle : Bright red cock

19. *Hook* : 18 eyed
    Body : Peacock herl
    Hackle : Blue dun cock

20. *Hook* : 18 or 20 eyed
    Body : Flat gold tinsel
    Hackle : Red-brown cock

21.   Grey Midge
      Hook :   18 eyed
      Body :   Dubbed mole's fur
      Hackle :   Grizzle cock

22.   *Hook* :   20 or 22, to gut, sneck,
                     blued
      Body :   Black silk
      Hackle :   Black cock, or hen

23.   *Hook* :   000 (18) to gut sneck, blued
      Tail :   A few strands of red seal's
                     fur
      Body :   Black seal's fur, ribbed 4 turns stripped hackle stalk

Long Legged Gnat

A favourite pattern of Roger Woolley and one he advised to be 'held handy by the flyfisher' in various colours. Gnats can be fished wet or dry and are taken by fish throughout the season. They are to be seen hovering in clouds over the water, and are often found to be more effective than normal dry fly on the quieter reaches of water. Dressings given in *Modern Trout Fly Dressing* use hackles twice the length of the body to suggest the legs of the insects. The dressing below has additional pheasant tail fibres tied in after the fashion of a Hawthorn Fly. It is possibly a development of the Long Legged Gnat.

1.   *Hook* :   2 eyed
      Silk :   Black
      Body :   Bronze peacock herl twisted with the silk, kept thin
      Legs :   Tied in at the thorax. Cock pheasant tail fibres clipped quarter
                     inch after the bend
      Hackle :   Dark dun cock

2.   Tailey Tail
     Hook :   1 eyed
     Tail :   Black cock hackle fibres
     Body :   Brown turkey
     Hackle :   Long black cock, 2 turns lying along the body base

Midge Doubles

Woolley tied up tiny doubles on hooks as small as 20 or even 22 (old numbers). At first these were tied to gut in a complex and difficult operation prior to adding the dressing. Later he used one eyed hook and one tapered shank hook binding them together tightly with silk and then easing them apart at an angle of 45 degrees using his thumbnail (*Modern Trout Fly Dressing*). He preferred these to a brazed double, believing them to be more flexible when a fish was hooked. Advantages of these doubles were better hooking and a small, though quick sinking, fly pattern.

The method of dressing is, to all intents and purposes, identical to that described by E M Tod in *Wet Fly Fishing* published in 1903. Woolley had Tod's approval to dress his patterns for sale and it would appear Woolley adopted the process to tie up his own chosen flies.

1.   *Hook* :   Smaller than 000, (20 - 22) double hook, eyed, bronzed
     Whisks :   3 x body length, Greenwell cock fibres
     Body :   Yellow silk, ribbed gold wire
     Hackle :   Greenwell cock
     Wing :   Blackbird or dark starling clipped at apex

Duns

1. March Brown
    Hook :   1 to gut, sneck
    Body :   Pale blue dun feather fibre,
                  palmered medium red cock
                  hackle, ribbed 4 turns fine
                  gold oval
    Hackle :   Medium red cock
    Wing :   Full, upright, pale hen
                  pheasant or woodcock wing
                  quill
    *(When dressing March Browns Woolley
    always recommended orange silk.)*

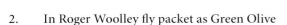

2. In Roger Woolley fly packet as Green Olive
    Hook :   1 to gut, bronze
    Tail :   Cinnamon feather fibre, long but clipped square
    Body :   Sage-coloured floss silk, ribbed 4 turns oval gold tinsel
    Wing :   Bronze mallard clipped square, level with hook bend

3. *Hook* :   0 to gut
    Body :   Pale blue dun feather fibre, palmered ginger cock hackle, ribbed
                  5 turns fine gold oval
    Hackle :   Light red cock
    Wing :   Upright, corncrake or cinnamon hen feather fibre

    *(The two dressings above are very similar in appearance, apart from the
    wing which is much fuller on the March Brown).*

4. *Hook* :   00 to gut, blued
    Whisks :   As hook length, 3 blue dun cock hackle fibres
    Body :   Yellow silk or floss, ribbed 4 turns fine gold oval
    Hackle :   Ginger cock
    Wing :   Pale grey starling, cinnamon cast in light (may be corncrake)

5.   *Hook* :   00 to gut
      Body :   Pale cinnamon or ginger fur dubbing
      Hackle :   Ginger cock
      Wing :   Upright, cinnamon quill fibre - may be corncrake

6.   *Hook* :   000 to gut
      Whisks :   Long, 3 blue dun cock fibres
      Body :   Flat gold tinsel
      Hackle :   Blue dun cock
      Wing :   Upright, pale starling

7.   *Hook* :   000 to gut
      Body :   Tied short, pale grey fur, hare or seal's
      Hackle :   Pale blue dun cock, 2 turns
      Wing :   Upright, pale starling

8.   *Hook* :   000 eyed
      Whisks :   Red ibis
      Body :   Sky blue floss silk, ribbed 5 turns silver wire
      Hackle :   Pale blue dun
      Wing :   Pale starling wing fibre

9.   *Hook* :   00 to gut
      Body :   Purple floss, ribbed 4 turns blue dun feather fibre
      Hackle :   Black hen
      Wing :   Upright, pale starling

10. Blue Dun

      Hook :   000 eyed, sneck
      Whisks :   Blue dun cock hackle fibres
      Body :   Dubbed mole, ribbed 4 turns yellow silk
      Hackle :   Blue dun cock
      Wing :   Full, upright, starling

11. *Hook* :   1 eyed
     Silk :   Crimson
     Whisks :   3 dun cock hackle
     Tip :   Crimson silk or floss
     Body :   Blue dun dubbing, probably stained seal's fur
     Hackle :   Stained blue cock
     Wing :   Medium starling

12. Cockwinged Dun
     Hook :   00 to gut, sneck
     Tip :   Yellow silk
     Body :   Blue dun fur, ribbed 3 turns yellow silk
     Hackle :   Cream or pale blue dun cock
     Wing :   Upright, pale starling

13. *Hook* :   000 eyed, sneck
     Silk :   Red
     Body :   Brown turkey fibre
     Wing :   Upright, dark brown feather quill

14. *Hook* :   000 to gut, sneck, blued
     Whisks :   Long, 3 times hook, 3
                   ginger cock hackle fibres
     Body :   Grey fur, possibly hare's
                   ear, dubbed tightly
     Hackle :   Medium red cock
     Wing :   Starling

15. Red Quill
     Hook :   00 to gut, sneck
     Whisks :   3 red cock hackle fibres
     Body :   Stripped peacock quill, 6-7 turns
     Hackle :   Full, red cock
     Wing :   Light starling

16.   *Hook* :   00 to gut
       Whisks :   3 Pale blue dun or white cock hackle fibres
       Body :   Primrose silk, ribbed 3 turns fine gold oval
       Hackle :   Ginger cock
       Wing :   Pale starling

17.   *Hook* :   0 to gut
       Body :   Stripped peacock quill, 7-8 turns
       Hackle :   Blue dun cock
       Wing :   Full, upright, starling

18.   *Hook* :   1 to gut
       Whisks :   2 or 3 Dark brown or black cock hackle fibres
       Body :   Dark blue dun floss
       Hackle :   Black hen
       Wing :   Hen pheasant or woodcock wing quill

19.   *Hook* :   00 to gut
       Body :   Chestnut floss, ribbed 5 turns gold wire
       Hackle :   Medium red cock
       Wing :   Dark hen pheasant wing quill, possibly grouse tail

20.   *Hook* :   3 to gut, japanned
       Body :   Straw floss
       Hackle :   Medium red cock
       Wing :   Dark starling

21.   *Hook* :   4 to gut, japanned
       Tip :   Flat gold tinsel
       Tail :   Golden pheasant tippets
       Body :   Stripped peacock quill
       Hackle :   Dun hen
       Wing :   'Cloudy' woodcock quill fibre

The following dressing is almost identical to that in *Modern Trout Fly*

Dressing. A gold tip has been added but this is something Roger Woolley often did with his dressings of Olives. He was sure this gave an 'edge' to certain flies. The hook size is much larger than the quoted size 0 in *Modern Trout Fly Dressing.*

22.   Apple Green Dun style
- *Hook :*   5 to gut, japanned
- *Tip :*   Gold silk
- *Body :*   Apple green floss
- *Hackle :*   Medium red cock
- *Wing :*   Medium starling

23.   *Hook :*   2 to gut
- *Body :*   Claret silk
- *Hackle :*   Light red cock
- *Wing :*   Black feather white tipped

24.   Rough Olive
- *Hook :*   2 eyed
- *Whisks :*   Olive stained cock hackle fibres
- *Body :*   Hare's ear fur, ribbed 4 turns gold oval
- *Hackle :*   Olive stained cock
- *Wing :*   Medium starling

25.   *Hook :*   2 eyed
- *Whisks :*   Cock hackle fibres stained red
- *Body :*   Claret seal's fur, ribbed 4 turns gold wire
- *Hackle :*   Cock, stained claret
- *Wing :*   'Cloudy' grey-white wing quill fibre

26.   *Hook :*   2 eyed
- *Whisks :*   Brown speckled partridge
- *Body :*   Red-brown feather herl, ribbed 3 turns gold wire
- *Hackle :*   Medium red cock
- *Wing :*   Medium starling

27. Cockwing Dun
    Hook :   2 up-eyed
    Whisks :   Pale yellow stained cock
    Body :   Primrose silk, ribbed 4 turns gold wire
    Hackle :   Bushy, cock stained pale yellow
    Wing :   Starling tied pent
    In Roger Woolley fly packet as Moss's Cockwing

28. *Hook* :   3 down-eyed bronzed
    Whisks :   Pale blue dun cock hackle fibres
    Body :   Dull yellow seal's fur
    Hackle :   Medium blue dun hen. Another in the same packet has a very dark blue dun hen hackle
    Wing :   Upright, pale starling wing quill fibre
    In Roger Woolley fly packet as Large Alder

29. *Hook* :   4 up eye bronzed
    Body :   Bright bronze peacock herl dressed tight and narrow
    Wing :   Brown speckled woodcock feather tied low over the body
    Hackle :   Long, black hen tied forward of wing in a ruff
    (This pattern could also be used as a dry fly. In Modern Trout Fly Dressing *'well worn' peacock herl is recommended when dressing Alders).*

30. *Hook* :   2, down-eyed, sneck
    Whisks :   Medium red cock hackle fibres
    Body :   Mole or dark grey fur, ribbed 4 turns gold wire
    Hackle :   2, speckled cock and dark red cock
    Wing :   Dark brown speckled feather tips, possibly grouse or woodcock

General and Fancy Wet Flies

Grouse wing

1. *Hook* : 00 eyed
   Tip : Gold floss
   Body : Bushy, bronze peacock herl
   Hackle : Cock, stained red, 3 turns
   Wing : Grouse fibre

2. *Hook* : 1 eyed
   Whisks : Light red hackle cock hackle fibres
   Body : Grey feather fibre, ribbed 3 turns oval gold
   Hackle : Dark speckled cock with red cock over
   Wing : Grouse hackle

3. Grouse and Claret
   Hook : 1 to gut, japanned
   Whisks : Golden pheasant tippets, long
   Body : Claret seal's fur, ribbed 3 turns oval gold tinsel
   Hackle : Cock, stained claret
   Wing : Grouse wing quill fibre

4. *Hook* : 2 to gut bronzed
   Tail : Long, 2 golden pheasant tippets
   Body : Dubbed hare's ear fur, ribbed 3 turns fine round gold tinsel
   Hackle : Speckled partridge
   Wing : Partridge or pale grouse fibre

5. Grouse and Claret
   Hook : 4 to gut, japanned
   Whisks : Golden pheasant tippet fibres, long
   Body : Claret seal's fur, ribbed 3 turns gold oval
   Thorax : Crimson seal's fur
   Wing : Speckled grouse fibres

6.   *Hook* :   4 to gut, japanned
     Whisks :   Cock hackle fibres,
                          stained red
     Body :   Orange seal's fur,
                   ribbed 3 turns flat
                   gold tinsel
     Hackle :   Greenwell hen
     Wing :   Speckled grouse tail fibre

7.   *Hook* :   5 to gut, japanned
     Body :   Magenta or crimson floss silk
     Hackle :   Dark brown hen
     Wing :   Grouse wing quill fibre

8.   *Hook* :   6 to gut, japanned
     Body :   Orange floss silk
     Hackle :   Woodcock or pale grouse
     Wing :   Speckled grouse or turkey

Pheasant wing

Hen pheasant and woodcock feather fibre are difficult to separate, especially in old material.

1.   Governor
     Hook :   1 to gut
     Tip :   Yellow or gold floss
     Body :   Bronze-magenta peacock herl
     Hackle :   Bright red cock
     Wing :   Hen pheasant or woodcock wing quill

2. *Hook* :   2 to gut
    Whisks :   Golden pheasant tippets
    Body :   Bottle-green floss, ribbed 3 turns flat silver tinsel
    Hackle :   Black cock
    Wing :   Woodcock or 'cloudy' hen pheasant tail wing quill

3. *Hook* :   5 to gut, japanned
    Body :   Amber seal's fur, thin and sparse
    Hackle :   Blue dun cock, sparse
    Wing :   Hen pheasant wing quill

4. *Hook* :   5 to gut, blued, sneck
    Tag :   Flat gold tinsel
    Body :   Black floss silk, palmered light red cock hackle
    Wing :   Pale, 'cloudy' hen pheasant wing quill fibre; paired and upright

5. *Hook* :   5 to gut, japanned
    Tip :   2 turns gold oval followed by orange floss
    Body :   Claret seal's fur, ribbed 4 turns oval gold tinsel
    Hackle :   Cock, stained claret
    Wing :   Hen pheasant tail fibre

6. Invicta
    Hook :   5 ls x 2 eyed
    Whisks :   Golden pheasant topping
    Body :   Amber seal's fur, palmered sparse red cock hackle, ribbed 5 turns gold oval
    Hackle :   Red cock, overlaid with long blue jay
    Wing :   Hen pheasant tail, pattern matched on both wings

7. | *Hook* : | 5 to gut, blued |
    | *Tag* : | Yellow floss silk |
    | *Tail* : | Golden pheasant tippet fibres |
    | *Body* : | Fiery-brown seal's fur |
    | *Hackle* : | Blue jay |
    | *Wing* : | Dark speckled hen pheasant tail or grouse tail |
    | *Head* : | Black varnish |

8. | *Hook* : | 5 to gut, japanned |
    | *Tail* : | Hen pheasant tail fibres, long |
    | *Body* : | Grey wool, ribbed 5 turns oval silver tinsel |
    | *Hackle* : | Speckled brown hen pheasant |
    | *Wing* : | Hen pheasant tail fibre |

9. | *Hook* : | 5 or 6 to gut, japanned |
    | *Body* : | Duck egg blue floss silk, palmered with black cock hackle, ribbed 5 turns flat gold tinsel |
    | *Hackle* : | Black cock |
    | *Wing* : | 'Cloudy' grey-white hen pheasant wing or woodcock fibre, paired |

10. | *Hook* : | 6 to gut, sneck |
    | *Body* : | Peacock herl butt, cream floss silk |
    | *Hackle* : | Light red cock |
    | *Wing* : | Pale hen pheasant tail, cream base with 'cloudy' speckles |

11. | *Hook* : | 6 to gut, japanned |
    | *Body* : | Half dirty orange seal's fur, half pea green seal's fur; ribbed 4 turns oval gold tinsel |
    | *Hackle* : | Only stubs remain – possibly dark brown or black |
    | *Wing* : | Hen pheasant tail fibre, paired |

12. *Hook* :   6 to gut, japanned
     Tail :   Chrome yellow feather fibre
     Body :   Purple floss silk, ribbed 5 turns oval silver tinsel
     Hackle :   Black hen
     Wing :   Hen pheasant tail fibre

13. *Hook* :   6 to gut, japanned
     Tip :   Gold floss silk
     Tail :   Golden pheasant tippet fibres and speckled mallard fibres
     Body :   Fiery-brown seal's fur, ribbed 5 turns oval gold tinsel
     Hackle :   Medium red cock
     Wing :   Hen pheasant tail fibre, paired

14. *Hook* :   6 to gut, japanned
     Tail :   Red ibis or red stained feather fibre
     Body :   Grass green wool, ribbed 4 turns flat gold tinsel
     Hackle :   Greenwell cock
     Wing :   Dark hen pheasant tail or grouse fibre

15. *Hook* :   7 to gut, japanned
     Whisks :   Cock pheasant tail fibres, long
     Body :   Buff dubbing, ribbed 6 turns silver wire
     Hackle :   Brown partridge
     Wing :   Pale hen pheasant tail fibre, paired; or possibly woodcock wing
                   quill fibre

16. *Hook* :   7 or 8 down-eyed bronze
     Tail :   Golden pheasant tippet
     Body :   Orange seal's fur, ribbed 5 turns gold oval tinsel
     Hackle :   Red hen
     Wing :   Hen pheasant tail

Cinnamon hen or Corncrake wing

Corncrake (or landrail) plumage was still available in the early days of Roger Woolley's career as a fly-dresser.

1. *Hook* :   2 to gut bronzed
    Tail :   2 Golden pheasant tippets
    Body :   Cinnamon wool
    Hackle : Medium red hen
    Wing :   Long, tied low, paired cinnamon feather fibre

2. *Hook* :   2 to gut, blued
    Body :   Orange floss silk, ribbed 4 turns oval gold tinsel
    Hackle : Black hen
    Wing :   Cinnamon hen or corncrake wing quill fibre

3. *Hook* :   4 to gut, japanned
    Whisks : Claret floss silk
    Body :   Claret floss silk, ribbed 4 turns flat gold tinsel
    Hackle : Black or dark claret cock
    Wing :   Cinnamon hen or corncrake inner, light bronze mallard cheeks

4. *Hook* :   4 or 5 to gut, japanned
    Body :   Bottle green floss silk, ribbed 4 turns flat gold tinsel
    Hackle : Black cock
    Wing :   Cinnamon hen quill or corncrake

5. *Hook* :   5 to gut, japanned
    Tail :   Golden pheasant topping
    Body :   Pale pink lamb's wool, palmered with light red cock hackle, ribbed 5 turns gold wire
    Hackle : Light red cock
    Wing :   Pale cinnamon quill fibre

6.   *Hook* :   7 to gut, japanned
        Body :   Orange-brown lamb's
                     wool, palmered red cock
                     hackle, ribbed 5 turns
                     oval gold tinsel
        Hackle :   Light red cock
        Wing :   Cinnamon hen quill fibre
                     or corncrake

7.   *Hook* :   7 to gut, japanned
        Body :   Orange-brown lamb's wool, ribbed 5 turns oval gold tinsel
        Hackle :   Medium red cock, long
        Wing :   Cinnamon quill fibre, 'cloudy'. Hen, corncrake or woodcock

White duck 'Satin' wing

1.   *Hook* :   1 to gut
        Body :   Rust silk
        Hackle :   Light red cock
        Wing :   White duck quill

2.   Coachman
        Hook :   2 to gut, sneck, blued
        Silk :   Red
        Body :   Bushy, bronze peacock herl
        Hackle :   Bright red cock, 3 turns
        Wing :   Upright, long, white duck quill

3.   *Hook* :   6 to gut, japanned
        Tail :   Crimson feather fibre, possibly ibis,
                     one-and-a-half times hook length
        Body :   Scarlet seal's fur, ribbed
                     4 turns flat gold tinsel
        Hackle :   Cock, stained scarlet
        Wing :   White duck quill, stained sky blue, upright

4.　*Hook* :　　6 to gut, japanned
　　Tag :　　Flat silver tinsel
　　Body :　　White chenille
　　Wing :　　Duck wing quill fibre,
　　　　　　　　stained scarlet; or red
　　　　　　　　ibis feather fibre, paired

Grey mallard quill wing

1.　*Hook* :　　4 to gut, japanned
　　Body :　　Two thirds yellow seal's fur, one third red seal's fur
　　Hackle :　　Light red cock
　　Wing :　　Grey mallard wing quill

2.　*Hook* :　　4 to gut, japanned
　　Body :　　Pink-bronze mixed seal's fur, bulky and carrot shaped
　　Hackle :　　Light red with an apricot cast, probably slightly stained
　　Wing :　　Grey-white mallard wing quill

3.　*Hook* :　　4 or 5 to gut, japanned
　　Body :　　Half orange seal's fur, half black seal's fur; ribbed 4 turns flat
　　　　　　　　gold tinsel
　　Hackle :　　Black hen
　　Wing :　　Blue-grey mallard wing quill

4.　*Hook* :　　5 to gut, japanned
　　Whisks :　　Bronze mallard fibres
　　Body :　　Sky blue wool, ribbed 4 turns silver wire
　　Hackle :　　Black hen
　　Wing :　　Grey mallard wing quill, only stubs remain

5. Cairns Fancy Style
    Hook :   6 to gut
    Whisks :   3 black cock fibres
    Body :   Sky blue floss, ribbed 5
                 turns silver wire
    Hackle :   Black cock
    Wing :   Grey mallard wing quill

6. *Hook* :   6 to gut, japanned
    Body :   Claret seal's fur, palmered 5 turns long red cock
    Hackle :   Possibly brown hen, otherwise absent
    Wing :   Grey mallard wing quill fibres

7. *Hook* :   6 to gut, japanned
    Tail :   Golden pheasant tippets
    Body :   Black ostrich herl, ribbed red cock hackle
    Hackle :   Red cock
    Wing :   Grey mallard wing quill fibres

8. *Hook* :   6 to gut, japanned
    Tail :   Red wool
    Body :   Black lamb's wool, ribbed 3 turns oval gold tinsel
    Hackle :   Black hen, sparse
    Wing :   Grey-blue dun mallard wing quill

9. *Hook* :   6 to gut, japanned
    Body :   Pale blue dun floss silk
    Hackle :   Dun hen, sparse
    Wing :   Grey mallard wing quill, lightly stained olive, sparse

10. *Hook* :   6 to gut, japanned
    Tail :   Grey mallard quill fibres
    Body :   One quarter primrose dubbing, three quarters Green
                    Highlander dubbing, ribbed 6 turns gold wire
    Hackle :   Medium red cock
    Wing :   Grey-white mallard wing quill

11. *Hook* :   6 to gut, japanned
    Tail :   Possibly mallard blue, but probably an exotic feather – electric,
                    iridescent blue fibres as in a macaw tail, slate grey back.
    Body :   Pink-pale violet floss silk, ribbed 6 turns fine oval gold tinsel
    Hackle :   Black hen
    Wing :   Smoky grey mallard quill

12. *Hook* :   7 to gut, japanned
    Tail :   Golden pheasant tippet
    Body :   Black seal's, ribbed 4 turns oval gold tinsel
    Hackle :   Blue jay
    Wing :   Grey mallard wing quill fibres

13. *Hook* :   7 to gut, japanned
    Butt :   Chestnut wool
    Body :   Peacock herl, tied short
    Hackle :   Blue dun cock
    Wing :   Grey-blue dun mallard wing quill

14. *Hook* :   7 to gut, japanned
    Body :   Half white floss silk, half red seal's fur, ribbed 4 turns
                    flat silver tinsel
    Hackle :   Greenwell cock, sparse
    Wing :   Grey-blue dun mallard wing quill

15.   *Hook* :   7 to gut, japanned
       Tail :   Golden pheasant tippets
       Body :   White floss silk, ribbed 5 turns flat silver tinsel
       Hackle :   Speckled brown-grey mallard
       Wing :   Blue-grey mallard wing quill

16.   *Hook* :   7 to gut, japanned
       Whisks :   Very long, golden pheasant tippets
       Body :   Primrose silk underbody leaving a tip, sparsely dubbed with blended cream and brown seal's fur, followed by dubbed black seal's thorax
       Hackle :   Dark dun cock
       Wing :   Smoky grey mallard quill

17.   *Hook* :   8 to gut, japanned
       Body :   Yellow seal's fur, ribbed 5 turns flat silver tinsel
       Hackle :   Medium red cock
       Wing :   Smoky grey mallard quill

Speckled grey mallard wing

1.   *Hook* :   3 to gut, bronzed
       Tail :   Brown speckled feather fibres, long
       Tip :   Flat gold tinsel
       Body :   Yellow-orange seal's fur; tied rather short
       Hackle :   Cock, stained orange
       Wing :   Speckled grey mallard fibres, stained olive

2. *Hook* :   5 to gut, blued, fine wire
    Whisks :   Black cock hackle fibres, long
    Body :   Peach floss silk, ribbed 5 turns silver wire
    Hackle :   Light red cock
    Wing :   Speckled grey mallard fibres

3. *Hook* :   6 eyed, japanned
    Tail :   Red feather fibre
    Body :   Claret seal's fur, ribbed oval gold tinsel, 4 turns
    Hackle :   Red cock
    Wing :   Grey-brown speckled mallard, full

4. *Hook* :   6 to gut, japanned
    Tag :   Chrome yellow feather fibre
    Body :   Fiery brown seal's fur, ribbed 4 turns oval gold tinsel
    Hackle :   Medium red cock
    Wing :   Speckled grey mallard fibre

5. *Hook* :   6 to gut, japanned
    Body :   Two thirds light yellow seal's fur, one third scarlet seal's fur,
                 ribbed 5 turns gold wire, tied rather short
    Hackle :   Black cock
    Wing :   Speckled grey mallard fibre, full

6. *Hook* :   6 to gut, blued, fine wire
    Body :   White lamb's wool, ribbed copper floss silk
    Hackle :   Light red cock
    Wing :   Speckled grey mallard, full

Crow quill wing

1. *Hook* :   4 to gut, sneck
    Body :   Amber seal's fur, ribbed 5 turns oval gold tinsel
    Hackle :   Black hen
    Wing :   Probably black crow quill fibre (absent except for stubs)

2. *Hook* :   4 to gut, japanned
    Body :   Sky blue floss silk, ribbed 8 turns silver wire
    Hackle :   Black hen
    Wing :   Probably black crow quill fibre (absent except for stubs)

Miscellaneous patterns

1. *Hook* :   0 to gut, japanned
    Body :   Crimson floss, ribbed 5 turns oval gold tinsel
    Hackle :   Cock, stained crimson
    Wing :   Paired jungle cock feathers low over body.

2. In Roger Woolley fly packet as Tups
    Hook :   1 down-eyed bronzed
    Whisks :   Brassy cock hackle fibres - these show a distinct yellowish sheen
                  and have sooty black butts
    Body :   3 or 4 turns of dull yellow silk at the tail followed by a tapered
                  body of seal's fur or wool mix containing buff-yellow and
                  orange fibres
    Hackle :   As whisks above, long with at least three turns
    (This fly is of the style described in Modern Trout Fly Dressing *as being
    suitable for use in the fast, rough waters of Devon as a wet fly).*

3. In Roger Woolley fly packet as Coch y bondu (sic)
    Hook :   2 down-eyed bronzed
    Body :   Bulky bronze peacock herl
    Hackle :   Long, full, furnace cock

4. *Hook* :   5 to gut, japanned
    Tail :   Feather fibre, stained dark red,
                long and sparse
    Body :   Red-brown lamb's wool,
                ribbed 5 turns yellow floss silk
    Hackle : Black hen
    Wing : Slate blue feather fibre, probably heron quill or crow

5. *Hook* :   5 to gut, japanned
    Tail :   Golden pheasant tippets
    Body :   Rich buff lamb's wool, ribbed 4 turns flat gold tinsel
    Hackle :   Medium red cock
    Wing :   Brown speckled partridge breast

6. *Hook* :   6 to gut, japanned
    Tail :   Yellow stained feather fibres
    Body :   Grey wool, ribbed 6 turns oval silver tinsel
    Wing :   Brown speckled cock fibres

7. Worm Fly
    Hooks :   2 eyed size 3. Dressed on gut, one on top the other at the point,
                 below. Each hook has a dressing applied
    Tails :   Red feather fibre
    Bodies :   Bronze peacock herl, bulky
    Hackles : Light red hen hackles, bushy

8. *Hook* :   5 to gut
    Body :   Scarlet floss silk
    Hackle :   Brown hen
    Wing :   Brown feather fibres

9. *Hook* :   6 down-eyed bronze
    Body :   Tapered, hare's ear fur dubbed on black silk, ribbed 5 turns oval
                 gold tinsel
    Hackle :   Full, dark blue dun cock

10. Stonefly Nymph
    Hook :   6 down-eyed silver
    Tail :   Brown feather fibres
    Body :   Carrot shaped, stripped peacock herl, brown and white
    Thorax :   Dirty cinnamon dubbing
    Legs, wing cases & antennae : Made from the same clip of buff
                 feather fibres bound in at front and rear of the thorax

Dry flies

1. Red Ant
   Hook :   000 down-eyed bronzed
   Body :   Orange-brown silk tied with bulbous body end and thorax and varnished over. This has created a pronounced waist on the fly and in addition, a striped effect on the body.
   Hackle :   Honey dun cock, 3 turns

2. In Roger Woolley fly packet as Iron Blue
   Hook :   000 up-eyed bronzed
   Whisks :   Long, 3 x body length, dark blue dun cock
   Body :   Mole fur, ribbed 4 turns full yellow or orange silk
   Hackle :   Dark blue dun cock
   Wing :   Upright, paired blackbird

3. *Hook* :   00 up-eyed bronzed
   Whisks :   Long, 2 x body length, blue dun cock
   Body :   Thin, claret silk
   Hackle :   Rusty blue dun cock
   Wing :   Pent, single, cream-dun feather fibre
   (This pattern is close to the Oakden's Claret dressing).

4. In Roger Woolley fly packet as Rough Olive
   Hook :   00 up-eyed bronzed
   Whisks :   Pale blue dun cock hackle fibres
   Body :   Heron herl, ribbed gold wire
   Hackle :   Pale blue dun cock
   Wing :   Upright, paired, dark starling
   (This dressing gives a much paler and delicate shade of the Rough Olive than those in Modern Trout Fly Dressing*).*

5.   In Roger Woolley fly packet as Red Quill
        Hook :   0 up-eyed bronzed
        Whisks :   Cock hackle fibres stained crimson
        Body :   Stripped peacock quill from eye, stained scarlet, (others
                         crimson)
        Hackle :   Red cock
        Wing :   Medium to dark starling

6.   In Roger Woolley fly packet as Sedge Fly
        Hook :   1 up-eyed bronzed
        Body :   Red-brown cock pheasant tail fibres, ribbed 3 turns round gold
                         tinsel
        Body hackle : Medium red cock
        Hackle :   As above tied bushy
        Wing :   Corncrake or cinnamon hen wing quill fibre

7.   In Roger Woolley fly packet as Cowdung Fly
        Hook :   3 up-eyed bronzed
        Body :   Dirty yellow lamb's wool
        Hackle :   Ginger cock
        Wing :   Corncrake or cinnamon hen wing quill fibre

8.   Daddy Long Legs
        Hook :   1 ls x 2 up-eyed
        Body :   Natural raffia, ribbed 4 turns gold wire or fine gold tinsel
        Legs :   6, double knotted feather fibres, probably fine dark cock
                         pheasant tail
        Hackle :   Rusty blue dun cock
        Wings :   Pale cree cock hackles dressed partially upright
        *(The dressing of this fly is very fine and delicate, giving the impression of
        one of the smaller species of crane fly but it was supplied in a number of
        sizes, probably to order. Roger Woolley refers to this fly being called by
        some anglers, 'Woolley's Deadly Daddy').*

9. Bluebottle
    Hook :   2 down-eyed
    Body :   Iron blue seal's fur, ribbed 3 turns fine flat silver tinsel
    Hackle :   Black cock
    Head :   Pale orange dubbing

10. Wickham's Fancy
    Hook :   5 eyed
    Whisks :   Bunch, red cock
    Body :   Flat gold tinsel, palmered red cock hackle, ribbed 5 turns oval
                 gold tinsel
    Collar hackle : Red cock
    Wing :   Dark grey mallard quill
    This fly is referred to in early catalogues as the Large Wickham.

11. Daddy Long Legs
    Hook :   7 sneck down-eyed
    Body :   Olive floss silk, carrot shaped
    Legs :   8 paired cock pheasant tail fibres, knotted once halfway down
                 their length to create 4 legs. Tied in between body and thorax
    Thorax :   Ball shaped, blue-green seal's fur
    Hackle :   Rich brown cock hackle tied full
    *(The green body and turquoise thorax of this dressing were evidently
    found useful by Roger Woolley long before the contemporary trend of
    tying Daddies with fluorescent green bodies).*

12. Soldier beetle style but grey-brown in colour
    Hook :   5 ls x 2 down-eyed
    Abdomen & thorax : Peacock herl with grey-dun feather fibre bound over
                 to form the wing cases and thorax
    Legs :   6, two emerge from the rear sides of the abdomen, two from the
                 front of the abdomen and two from the thorax. Broad grey-
                 brown goose feather fibre
    Head :   Prominent, black
    (The fly may not be a conventional dry fly but would certainly float if dressed).

Fan winged mayflies

Writing of the artificial mayfly in *The Fly-Fisher's Flies*, 1938, Roger Woolley remarked that the mallard-winged patterns were now out of date. He considered that where a winged dressing was required, the hackle-fibre winged-fly style of John Henderson was taking its place, offering significant advantages of durability and buoyancy. Despite this, Woolley said that in his experience the simpler hackle-winged flies were the favourites. Whether the favourites of angler or fish he does not detail, but then it would amount to much the same thing.

1. The Fisher for Windermere
   - *Hook* : 4 ls x 2 eyed
   - *Body* : Cream raffia, ribbed 5 turns red cock hackle and yellow silk
   - *Hackle* : Brown speckled cock
   - *Wing* : Fan, grouse covert or breast

2. Costa No. 1
   - *Hook* : 1 ls x 2 eyed, bronzed
   - *Whisks* : 3 hen pheasant tail fibres or speckled cock
   - *Body* : Wheat straw, ribbed 3 turns each olive floss and oval gold tinsel
   - *Hackle* : Grizzle cock, stained yellow
   - *Wing* : Fan, speckled grey mallard
   - *Head* : Green peacock herl

3. Costa No. 2
   - *Hook* : 1 ls x 2 eyed, bronzed
   - *Whisks* : Hen pheasant tail fibres or speckled cock
   - *Body* : White floss, ribbed 6 turns oval gold tinsel
   - *Hackle* : Dark speckled grizzle cock
   - *Wing* : Fan, Speckled grey mallard stained yellow or wood duck, clipped to shape
   - *Head* : Green peacock herl

4. Costa No. 3
   - *Hook* : 1 ls x 2 eyed, bronzed
   - *Whisks* : 3 hen pheasant tail fibres or speckled cock
   - *Body* : White floss, ribbed 6 turns oval gold tinsel
   - *Hackle* : Light grizzle cock
   - *Wing* : Fan, bright yellow stained, speckled grey mallard stained bright yellow or wood duck, clipped to shape
   - *Head* : Bronze peacock herl

The Costa Beck in Yorkshire

Costa numbers 2 and 3 are very similar to one another; the differences really being a matter of shades. Since Woolley had gone to the unusual trouble of giving them specific labels he must have considered the stresses important. If nothing else, all three patterns are very delicate and attractive, being dressed on small hooks compared to most of the other patterns.

These three flies were, in all likelihood, dressed to fish the Costa Beck, a small spring-fed limestone river near Malton in Yorkshire. Not far from here, in Scarborough, Roger Woolley had relatives. T E Pritt, writing in *The Book of the Grayling* in 1888, refers to the River Costa as 'the best Yorkshire grayling river' and as being 'not dissimilar to the Derbyshire rivers.' If this was still the case some years later, the attraction of the Costa to Roger Woolley requires no explanation. Writing in *Country Life Library of Sport – Fishing*, R B Marston describes the Costa as having 'much of the nature of a south-country chalk stream.' He reports seeing grayling of between two and four pounds in weight, but adds 'that since other lures besides the artificial fly have been allowed the fish have sadly deteriorated both in size and number.' These remarks were made in 1904. Marston also records that the river had 'a grand supply of fresh-water shrimp at that time.'

A significant number of the fan-winged patterns are dressed on large hooks and have huge wings. As such they would be formidable flies to cast accurately and so are perhaps intended for use as dapping flies.

5. *Hook* : 5 ls x 2 to gut
    Body : Buff woven thread or worsted, ribbed 4 turns black floss
    Hackle : Light red and speckled brown cock
    Wing : Fan, speckled grey mallard
    Head : Peacock herl

6. *Hook* : 5 ls x 2 to gut
    Whisks : 4 buff cock hackle fibres
    Body : Wheat straw, ribbed 4 turns red-brown silk, varnished
    Hackle : Well-marked speckled cream and brown cock
    Wing : Fan, large speckled grey mallard
    Head : Peacock herl

7. *Hook* : 3 ls x 2 to gut
    Whisks : 3 long speckled cream and brown cock or speckled turkey
    Body : Wheat straw, ribbed 5 turns red silk and gold oval
    Hackle : Red and speckled brown cock
    Wing : Fan, speckled grey mallard, stained olive
    Head : Peacock herl

8. *Hook* :   2 ls x 2 to gut, sneck, bronze
    Whisks : 4 black cock hackle fibres
    Tip :   Red silk
    Body :   Wheat straw, ribbed 3 turns red
                silk varnished
    Hackle : Light red cock
    Wing :   Fan, speckled grey mallard,
                stained light olive
    Head :   Bronze peacock herl

9. *Hook* :   3 ls x 2 to gut
    Whisks : 3 dark cock hackle fibres
    Body :   Buff chenille palmered light red cock
    Hackle : Buff speckled cock
    Wing :   Fan, grey speckled mallard

10. *Hook* :   5 ls x 2 to gut
    Whisks : Black cock hackle fibres
    Body :   White floss or wool, palmered 9 turns red cock hackle
    Wing :   Fan, speckled grey mallard

11. *Hook* :   5 ls x 2 to gut
    Tip :   Red-brown silk
    Body :   Cream floss, ribbed 4 turns red-brown silk
    Hackle : Medium red cock
    Wing :   Fan, speckled grey mallard, stained olive

12. *Hook* :   7 to gut, japanned
    Whisks : Black cock hackle fibres
    Body :   Primrose seal's fur, palmered yellowish hackle
    Hackle : 2 ginger cock
    Wing :   Fan, buff speckled mallard
    Head :   Peacock herl

13. *Hook* :   5 to gut
     Butt :   Peacock herl
     Body :   Cream floss, palmered red cock hackle
     Hackle :   2 ginger cock
     Wing :   Grey speckled mallard
     Head :   Peacock herl

14. *Hook* :   3 or 4 to gut
     Whisks :   Black cock hackle fibres
     Body :   Cream wool, ribbed rusty silk
     Hackle :   Dark red cock
     Wing :   Fan, grey speckled mallard
     Head :   Green peacock herl

15. *Hook* :   4 ls x 2 to gut
     Whisks :   3 cock pheasant tail fibres
     Body :   Wheat straw, ribbed 5 turns yellow silk
     Hackle :   Speckled cock, stained yellow
     Wing :   Fan, grey speckled mallard
     Head :   Peacock herl

16. *Hook* :   6 ls x 2 to gut
     Whisks :   Speckled turkey or bronze mallard fibres
     Body :   Cream floss, palmered 5 turns red cock hackle
     Hackle :   Red cock
     Wing :   Fan, speckled grey mallard

17. *Hook* :   1 ls x 3 to gut, sneck
     Whisks :   3 cock pheasant tail fibres
     Body :   Wheat straw ribbed 5 turns hackle stalk
     Hackle :   Speckled cock, stained yellow
     Wing :   Fan, cock, stained yellow
     Head :   Green peacock herl

18. *Hook* :   9 to gut
     Whisks :   Dark cock hackle fibres
     Body :   Cork strip, palmered 5 turns badger cock hackle
     Hackle :   Brown speckled cock
     Wing :   Fan, speckled grey mallard

19. *Hook* :   7 to gut
     Whisks :   3 speckled turkey fibres
     Body :   Natural lamb's wool,
                   ribbed 7 turns light red
                   cock hackle, clipped
     Hackle :   Bushy, speckled dun cock
     Wing :   Fan, large, teal flank
     Head :   Peacock herl

20. *Hook* :   6 to gut, sneck
     Whisks :   Brown cock hackle fibres
     Body :   Blue dun wool, ribbed 6 turns brown silk
     Hackle :   Brown speckled grouse or pheasant covert
     Wing :   Fan, teal flank

21. *Hook* :   6 to gut, sneck
     Whisks :   Black hackle fibres
     Body :   Wheat straw, ribbed 6 turns brown silk
     Hackle :   Light red cock
     Wing :   Fan, pale teal flank
     Head :   Peacock herl

22. *Hook* :   7 ls x 2 to gut
     Body :   Buff wool, palmered ginger cock hackle
     Hackle :   Ginger cock
     Wing :   Fan, pale teal flank
     Head :   Peacock herl

23. *Hook* : 8 ls x 2 to gut
    Whisks : 3 cock pheasant tail fibres
    Body : Natural lamb's wool
    Hackle : Bushy; red speckled cock and speckled grey mallard
    Wing : Fan, teal flank, stained yellow

24. *Hook* : 5 ls x 2 to gut
    Whisks : Grizzle cock hackle fibres
    Body : Wheat straw, palmered grizzle cock hackle
    Hackle : Grizzle cock
    Wing : Fan, pale teal flank

25. *Hook* : 1 ls x 2 to gut
    Whisks : Brown speckled cock hackle fibres
    Body : Cream raffia, ribbed 5 turns brown silk
    Hackle : Red cock and grizzle cock
    Wing : Fan, mallard stained yellow; or wood duck
    Head : Peacock herl

26. *Hook* : 7 ls x 2 to gut
    Body : Tup's wool, ribbed 4 turns pink silk
    Hackle : Ginger cock
    Wing : Fan, pale speckled buff cock

27. *Hook* : 7 ls x 2 to gut, sneck
    Body : White wool
    Hackle : White cock
    Wing : Fan, pure white duck
    Hook : 5 eyed
    Whisks : Speckled turkey or bronze mallard fibres
    Body : Wheat straw, ribbed 4 turns yellow silk
    Hackle : Yellow stained, speckled cock
    Wing : Fan, white duck

28. *Hook* :   5 eyed
    Whisks :   Speckled turkey or bronze mallard fibres
    Body :   Wheat straw ribbed 4 turns yellow silk
    Hackle :   Yellow stained speckled cock
    Wing :   Fan white duck

29. *Hook* :   5 eyed
    Whisks :   Black cock hackle fibres
    Body :   Peach floss, ribbed black silk
    Hackle :   Buff cock and dark brown cock
    Wing :   Fan, teal flank
    Head :   Peacock herl

30. *Hook* :   5 ls x 3 eyed
    Whisks :   Cock pheasant tail fibres
    Body :   White floss, ribbed 4 turns
         black floss evenly spaced
    Body Hackle : Red cock, 4 turns
    Hackle :   Red cock and mallard
         stained yellow
    Wing :   Fan, large, mallard stained yellow-olive

31. *Hook* :   5 ls x 2 eyed
    Whisks :   Black whiskers
    Body :   Wheat straw, ribbed 4 turns claret silk
    Hackle :   Red cock
    Wing :   Fan, small, grey mallard

32. *Hook* :   2 ls x 2 eyed
    Whisks :   Black whiskers
    Tip :   Black silk
    Body :   Wheat straw, ribbed 4 turns medium red cock hackle
    Hackle :   Medium red cock
    Wing :   Fan, grey speckled mallard stained yellow
    Head :   Green peacock herl

33.   *Hook* :   2 ls x 2 eyed
         Whisks :   3 speckled turkey or bronze mallard fibres
         Body :   White floss, ribbed 5 turns red cock hackle
         Hackle :   Medium red cock with brown speckled partridge over
         Wing :   Fan, large, speckled grey mallard stained olive

34.   *Hook* :   4 ls x 2 to gut
         Whisks :   3 brown speckled mallard fibres
         Tip :   Possibly red Lurex, or perhaps more likely tarnished tinsel
         Butt :   Peacock herl
         Body :   White floss, ribbed 3 turns flat silver tinsel
         Hackle :   Grouse wing covert
         Wing :   Fan, yellow stained speckled grey mallard

35.   *Hook* :   3 ls x 3 eyed
         Whisks :   3 speckled brown
                      mallard fibres
         Body :   Cream quill, ribbed 4
                      turns green floss and
                      fine oval gold tinsel
         Hackle :   Medium red cock
         Wing :   Fan, speckled grey mallard

36.   *Hook* :   4 ls x 3 eyed
         Tip :   Black silk
         Body :   Wheat straw, ribbed 4 turns black silk
         Hackle :   Short, ginger cock
         Wing :   Fan, speckled grey mallard stained dark olive, clipped to shape
         Head :   Peacock herl

37. *Hook* : 3 ls eyed
    Whisks : Mixed black and white whiskers
    Body : Brown material, appearance of a rubber band wrapped on the hook. Ribbed 5 turns oval silver tinsel.
    (Woolley sometimes used gut for bodies but the above material has an angular cross section).
    Hackle : Blue dun cock
    Wing : Fan, grouse wing coverts
    Head : Peacock herl

38. *Hook* : 1 ls x 2 eyed
    Whisks : 3 grizzle cock hackle fibres
    Body : Dirty white feather fibre, ribbed 4 turns ginger cock and possibly gold wire
    Hackle : Speckled grey mallard
    Wing : Fan, small grey speckled mallard

39. *Hook* : 3 ls x 2 eyed
    Whisks : Speckled turkey or bronze mallard fibres
    Body : Cream wheat straw, ribbed 5 turns red-brown silk
    Hackle : Red cock and speckled brown cock
    Wing : Fan, speckled grey mallard stained greenish-yellow; or possibly wood duck.

40. *Hook* : 3 ls x 2 eyed
    Whisks : 3 long brown cock pheasant tail fibres
    Body : Dark wheat straw, ribbed 5 turns brown silk
    Hackle : Bushy, medium red cock and speckled brown cock
    Wing : Fan, speckled grey mallard stained greenish-yellow; or wood duck

41. *Hook* : 3 ls x 2 eyed
    Whisks : Speckled grey mallard stained greenish-yellow; or wood duck
    Body : Primrose seal's fur, ribbed 3 turns rust silk
    Hackle : Speckled cock stained yellow
    Wing : Fan, speckled brown mallard stained greenish-yellow

42. *Hook* : 3 ls x 2 eyed
  Whisks : Speckled grey mallard
  Body : Raffia, ribbed 5 turns orange silk
  Hackle : Speckled red cock stained yellow
  Wing : Fan, speckled grey mallard stained olive

Several of the dressings with detached bodies have their wings clipped to shape; a practice Woolley deprecated in his writings. It is possible that fashion held sway over principle at times. He says there was very little demand for flies with detached bodies. Whilst they looked attractive and lifelike, due to the way they were constructed they were very stiff. Commercially-produced rubber bodies overcame this problem but were no more popular with anglers. A far more succulent-looking body was made from oiled silk material, often used for tobacco pouches, but evidently did not increase enthusiasm for the style of dressing.

When cork strip was used to wrap the body Woolley recommended that it should be varnished. The dressings listed below show little evidence of this but that may well be to do with deterioration over the years of storage.

43. *Hook* : 1 ls x 2 to gut
  Whisks : Brown speckled cock hackle fibres
  Body : Half detached, cork strip over a bunch of stiff bristles, ribbed 6 turns of brown silk
  Hackle : Brown speckled cock and red cock
  Wing : Fan, mallard stained yellow; or possibly wood duck

44. *Hook* : 1 to gut
  Whisks : 2 fine black whiskers
  Body : Detached, white cord, varnished, cross ribbed with yellow silk. Body detached and upturned from hook bend.
  Hackle : Light red cock
  Wing : Fan, speckled grey mallard stained yellow
  Head : Black varnish

45. *Hook* : 6 ls x 2, to gut, japanned
    Whisks : Brown speckled cock
    Body : Detached from hook bend. Appearance of fine clear cord, wrapped to produce ribbed effect
    Hackle : Ginger cock
    Wing : Bunched, speckled grey mallard
    Head : Bronze peacock herl

46. *Hook* : 1 ls x 2 to gut
    Whisks : 3 dark grizzle cock or bronze mallard
    Body : Detached from above the hook bend, based on a stripped hackle stalk, probably wrapped with oiled silk material, over yellow wool. The dressing has deteriorated now, giving the appearance of brown resin
    Hackle : Grizzle cock
    Wing : Fan, pale teal flank clipped to shape

47. *Hook* : 1 s x 2 eyed
    Whisks : 3 cock pheasant tail fibres
    Body : Detached from half way down hook bend, cork strip over bunch of stiff bristles ribbed 7 turns straw silk and spotted with brown mark on each segment
    Hackle : Blue dun cock
    Wing : Fan, bronze mallard clipped to shape
    Head : Peacock herl

48. *Hook* : 5 ls x 2 to gut, japanned
    Whisks : Cock pheasant tail fibres
    Body : Detached from hook bend; cork strip over bunch of stiff bristles, ribbed 6 turns brown silk, marked with black dots on segments
    Hackle : Light red cock
    Wing : Fan, speckled grey mallard trimmed to shape
    Head : Peacock herl

49.   *Hook* :   5 ls x 2 to gut
       Whisks :   3 Cock pheasant tail fibres
       Body :   Detached. Cream cork with applied marks to imitate segments, ribbed yellow silk, detached from hook bend. May be a commercially produced body.
       Hackle :   Red cock
       Wing :   Fan, speckled grey mallard

Detached body mayflies must have taken far more time to dress than other standard patterns. Price lists in the catalogues do not itemise them separately; presumably, in the absence of popular demand, a price would be quoted on request.

Feather quill tube Mayfly

1.   *Hook* :   None. The fly base consists of a piece of hollow, tapered feather quill 20 mm long
       Whisks : 3 cock pheasant tail fibres, 35 mm long
       Tip :   Red-brown silk, 5 close turns
       Body :   Natural quill, stained yellow-olive, ribbed 8 turns red brown silk – the quill colour may be yellow-green due to the varnish
       Hackle : Long, dirty yellow-buff tips with light brown list or base
       Wing :   Fan, large, speckled grey mallard stained
       It is interesting to speculate how this fly was fished. Was a treble hook used? Such recourse seems rather excessive. Maybe it was simply an experimental dressing, perhaps for the then new style of salmon fishing with dry fly.

C F Walker, in *Fly Tying as an Art*, includes a plate depicting a tube-bodied pattern under the title 'Some Freaks and Fancies'. He describes how he experimented with dressing such a fly using semi-transparent plastic tubing. The gut was to be passed through the body tubing and a short-shank, wide-gape hook tied on so 'no part of the hook was actually inside the fly'. He carried these flies when fishing but either 'mislaid' them (deliberately?) or found the fish happy with other, more 'normal', patterns. Consequently he did not trial them thoroughly. He does, however, mention an acquaintance, Mr R E H Drury, a skilled fly-dresser who had a similar idea years earlier and had considerable success with tube-bodied mayflies. No other details are given but it would appear quite a difficult operation to guarantee the single hook remaining in line without insertion into the body tube. The use of hollow feather quills such as Roger Woolley used is not mentioned. Maybe his trials came to nought too.

For those who wish to use fan wing patterns, Roger Woolley proffers the advice to replace the easily-waterlogged mallard and wood duck feathers with those from the outside of a cockerel's wing. Pale-coloured feathers with a brown speckle dyed yellow-olive are excellent substitutes.

Hackle-point mayflies

Whilst Roger Woolley thought hackle-point mayfly wings preferable to fan wings he comments on their chief disadvantage as that of tucking up under the bend of the hook and thereby ruining the presentation of the fly. This problem was best avoided, according to Woolley, by ensuring the wing length was no greater than the distance from eye to hook bend.

With the exceptions of honey dun and brassy dun cock hackles, natural colours of feathers do not lend themselves as material for mayfly wings. To solve this Woolley advocated slightly staining pale blue dun cock hackles in yellow dye. A useful range of olive shades is thereby produced.

1.   *Hook* :   4 ls x 3 eyed
       Whisks :   3 Speckled brown mallard fibres
       Body :   Split feather quill wrapped round hook, ribbed 4 turns peacock herl
       Hackle :   Pale blue dun or cream cock
       Wing :   4 hackle points, dun cock, spent

2.   *Hook* :   5 ls x 2 eyed
      Butt :   Bronze-magenta peacock herl
      Body :   White quill, ribbed black silk
      Hackle :   Grizzle cock
      Wing :   4 hackle points, blue dun cock

3.   *Hook* :   5 eyed
      Whisks :   Grizzle cock hackle fibres
      Body :   Dark grey floss or silk, ribbed green peacock sword
      Hackle :   Bushy black cock
      Wing :   4 hackle points, dun cock

4.   *Hook* :   3 ls x 2 to gut
      Whisks :   3 buff speckled cock hackle fibres
      Body :   Dark wheat straw, ribbed 5 turns oval gold tinsel
      Hackle :   Grizzle cock and medium red cock
      Wing :   4 hackle points stained olive
      Head :   Peacock herl

5.   *Hook* :   2 or 3 ls x 2 eyed
      Whisks :   3 brown-black cock
                    hackle fibres
      Tip :   Rich brown hackle stalk
      Body :   Dark cream raffia, ribbed 4 turns rich
                    brown hackle stalk
      Hackle :   Dun cock
      Wing :   4 hackle points,
                    dark dun cock, spent

6.   *Hook* :   2 ls x 2 eyed
      Body :   Natural raffia, ribbed 4 turns brown silk
      Hackle :   French partridge
      Wing :   4 hackle points, blue dun cock, spent

7. *Hook* : 2 ls x 2 eyed
   Whisks : Bronze mallard
   Body : Wheat straw, ribbed 3 turns brown silk
   Hackle : Red cock and French partridge
   Wing : 4 hackle points, speckled dun cock, spent

8. *Hook* : 2 ls x 2 eyed
   Whisks : 3 dark cock hackle fibres
   Tip : Red-brown silk
   Body : Raffia ribbed 4 turns brown silk, first wider
   Hackle : White cock and red brown cock

9. *Hook* : 2 ls x 2 eyed
   Whisks : Dark cock hackle fibres
   Body : Raffia, ribbed 4 turns brown silk, first wider
   Hackle : Speckled red-brown cock and grouse or woodcock hackle
   Wing : 4 hackle points, dark blue dun cock, spent

10. *Hook* : 2 ls x 2 eyed
    Whisks : Black cock hackle fibres
    Tip : Brown silk
    Body : Cream raffia, ribbed 5 turns brown silk
    Hackle : Dark dun cock
    Wing : 4 hackle points, dark dun cock, spent brown cock
    Wings : 4 hackle points, brassy dun cock, spent

11. *Hook* : 4 ls x 2 eyed
    Whisks : 3 dark speckled mallard fibres
    Body : White floss, ribbed 5 turns peacock herl and pale blue dun or
    white cock hackle
    Hackle : Grizzle cock
    Wing : 4 hackle points, dark blue dun, spent
    Head : Peacock herl

Hackled Mayflies

Roger Woolley, again writing in *The Fly-Fisher's Flies*, thought the best hackled patterns to be the Wood Duck, Major, Lawrence, Colonel and Black Drake. Both the Colonel and Wood Duck had been recommended in his catalogues for many years and had obviously stood the test of time in his experience and affections. He adds that the Spent Drake is essential, 'the fly-dresser will provide a good selection for choice'.

The Major may well be a fly dedicated to Roger Woolley's friend and fishing partner Major T H Oakden of Rolleston-on-Dove, but the dressing is not listed. Two other patterns, Tommy's Favourite and Oakden's Claret, were named for Oakden by Woolley.

Below are listed hackled mayflies dressed by Roger Woolley. Most are from his personal fly-case.

The Brailsford — The badly damaged original fly in Roger Woolley's fly book and on page 72 a copy tied by the author.

1. The Brailsford
   Hook :   3 ls x 2 eyed
   Whisks :   3 black whiskers or
               fibres
   Body :   White floss, ribbed 3
               turns Greenwell cock
               hackle
   Hackle :   Grizzle cock and
               speckled mallard
   (This example tied by the author)

Roger Woolley fished for trout on the Brailsford, Longford and Sutton Brooks, tributaries of the River Dove and just a few miles from his home in Hatton. His experiences on them were sufficient to name a pattern as a memento. Charles Cotton also mentions Brailsford Brook in his account of Viator and Piscator's journey from Derby to Beresford in *The Compleat Angler*.

2. *Hook* :   6 or 7 down-eyed bronzed
   Whisks :   Gold feather fibre, possibly stained white goose or duck
   Body :   One third scarlet floss, one third white floss, one third gold floss.
               The centre third ribbed 3 turns fine gold or silver tinsel
   Hackle :   Badger hen with grey speckled mallard or pale wood duck
               feather over. This feather is of a very pale yellow shade and may
               be stained

3. The Gedney No. 2
   Hook :   4 ls x 2 eyed
   Body :   Natural raffia, ribbed 6 turns gold wire
   Hackle :   Grizzle cock and speckled grey-buff mallard
   Head :   Green peacock herl

This pattern may have been named for, or been originated by, C W Gedney, a well-known angler on the Midland trout streams, and especially on the River Dove. Gedney wrote *Angling Holidays in Pursuit of Salmon, Trout and Pike* in 1896 and produced a short chapter (dealing with tackle, method and flies, and titled *Dry Fly Fishing*) for *The Scientific Angler,* written by David Foster of Ashbourne and published posthumously by his sons in 1882. Gedney makes no mention of mayflies, confining his remarks to a dozen or so patterns for the use of beginners to the art. He fished the waters of Ireland, Wales and Scotland in addition to the Trent, Darenth, Wiltshire Avon and Canterbury Stour. He and Woolley were contemporaries and it is likely they were well known to one another, both being regulars on the Dove. The Gedney No. 1 is not represented in the fly-case but was perhaps similar in style to the No. 2 with colour variations, as in the Costa series.

4. *Hook* :   1 ls x 2 down-eyed bronzed
    Whisks :   Absent, stubs only
    Butt :   Peacock herl
    Body :   Wheat straw, ribbed 4 turns scarlet floss silk and fine gold tinsel
    Hackle :   Medium red hen with wood duck or grey mallard stained
                  primrose over
    Head :   Peacock herl

5. *Hook* :   2 ls x 3 down-eyed reversed bronzed
    Whisks :   Dun cock hackle fibres
    Body :   Wheat straw, varnished, ribbed 4 turns round gold tinsel
    Hackle :   Orange stained cock with brown and white speckled mallard
                  over, slightly longer than hook length

6. *Hook* :   4 ls x 3 to gut
    Whisks :   Cock pheasant tail fibres
    Tip :   Black silk
    Body :   Wheat straw, ribbed 5 turns hackle stalk and green silk
    Hackle :   Light grey cock and speckled grey mallard

7. *Hook* :   6 eyed
    Whisks :   Black cock hackle fibres
    Body :   Cream chenille, ribbed peacock sword herl
    Hackle :   Dun cock

8. *Hook* :   3 ls x 3 down-eyed bronzed
    Whisks :   Long, rich brown and white feather fibre, possibly golden pheasant
    Body :   Natural raffia, ribbed 4 turns round gold tinsel
    Hackle :   Cock stained orange with long grey speckled mallard lightly
                 stained primrose
    *(Also a cock badger hackle now erect behind the other hackles, possibly a
    wing, probably a hackle which has come unwound).*

9. *Hook* :   3 ls x 2 eyed
    Whisks :   3 cock pheasant tail fibres
    Body :   Natural raffia, ribbed 5 turns orange silk and oval gold tinsel
    Hackle :   Blue dun cock hackle and greenish stained speckled mallard or
                 partridge, rather short and even

10. *Hook* :   3 ls x 2 up-eyed
    Whisks :   Speckled golden pheasant tail feather fibres
    Body :   Natural raffia, palmered with pale blue dun cock hackle, ribbed
                 4 turns oval silver tinsel
    Hackle :   Black cock, long and full

11. *Hook* :   4 ls x 2 up-eyed
    Whisks :   3 cock pheasant tail fibres
    Body :   White floss, palmered with pale cream cock hackle, ribbed 4
                 turns oval gold tinsel
    Hackle :   White cock with black cock hackle over

12. *Hook* :   4 ls x 2 up-eyed
    Whisks :   Black feather herl, probably crow wing or tail
    Body :   White floss, ribbed 5 turns oval silver tinsel
    Hackle :   Light red hen with speckled grey mallard over

13.   *Hook* :   4 ls x 2 up-eyed
      Whisks :   3 cock pheasant tail fibres
      Body :   Straw floss silk, ribbed 4 turns oval gold tinsel
      Hackle :   Pale blue dun cock with white cock over

14.   *Hook* :   4 ls x 2 down-eyed reversed
      Whisks :   3 red-brown cock pheasant tail fibres
      Body :   Buff wool or possibly seal's fur, ribbed 5 turns orange silk
      Hackle :   Badger hen with brown and white speckled mallard over, long
      Head :   Bronze peacock herl

15.   *Hook* :   2 ls x 2 down-eyed sneck bronzed
      Whisks :   Red-brown cock pheasant tail fibres
      Body :   White lamb's wool, ribbed 4 turns fine gold tinsel
      Hackle :   Badger hen, stained orange with barred French partridge over

16.   *Hook* :   4 ls x 2 eyed sneck, bronzed
      Whisks : 3 brown speckled fibres
      Butt :   Green peacock herl
      Body :   White lamb's wool, ribbed 5 turns gold oval tinsel
      Hackle : 3 red cock, speckled cock and very long speckled grey mallard stained yellow; or possibly Egyptian goose

17.   *Hook* :   5 ls x 3 eyed
      Whisks :   Cock pheasant tail fibres
      Butt :   Peacock herl
      Body :   Cream quill, ribbed 5 turns brown silk
      Hackle :   Brown speckled cock

18. **Hook**: 4 ls x 2 to gut
    Body: White lamb's wool, ribbed 5 turns black silk
    Hackle: Red cock and pale speckled grey mallard
    Head: Peacock herl

19. **Hook**: 5 down-eyed, sneck, bronzed
    Whisks: 3 black cock hackle fibres
    Body: White floss, ribbed 5 turns badger hackle, possibly over cork strip. (The latter emerges over the hook bend.)
    Hackle: Bushy, speckled cock with black cock in front

20. **Hook**: 3 ls x 2 eyed
    Whisks: 3 long red cock hackle fibres
    Butt: Green peacock herl
    Body: White or pale primrose lamb's wool, ribbed 4 turns oval gold tinsel
    Hackle: 2, ginger hen with speckled grey cock in front

21. **Hook**: 4 ls x 2 to gut
    Whisks: 3 cock pheasant tail fibres
    Body: Yellow herl, ribbed 4 turns gold wire
    Hackle: Stained bright yellow, grey speckled mallard

22. *Hook* :   3 ls x 3 eyed
     Whisks :   Speckled grey
                   mallard
     Butt :   Peacock herl
     Body :   Duck egg blue quill
                   or latex, ribbed 4
                   turns cream herl
                   and silver wire
     Hackle :   Very long, 3 times
                   hook, speckled
                   beige Egyptian
                   goose flank
                   or breast

23. *Hook* :   4 ls x 2 down-eyed
                   bronzed
     Whisks :   3 cock golden
                   pheasant tail fibres
     Body :   Brown or dark claret floss silk, ribbed 4 turns natural raffia
     Body Hackle : Bright red cock
     Hackle :   Red cock with a bushy and long dark brown,
                   yellow spotted hackle.
     (This could be guinea fowl stained yellow or an unknown exotic).

24. *Hook* :   3 ls x 2 eyed
     Whisks :   Black cock hackle fibres
     Body :   Raffia, ribbed 4 turns red-brown floss
     Hackle :   Mixed, teal, speckled grey mallard and red-brown cock

25. *Hook* :   3 ls x 3 eyed
     Whisks :   Black cock hackle fibres
     Body :   Yellow floss, ribbed 5 turns black floss
     Hackle :   Medium red cock and teal flank

26. *Hook* : 3 ls x 3 eyed
    Whisks : Black cock hackle fibres
    Body : White floss, ribbed 5 turns peacock herl
    Hackle : Bushy, black cock and French partridge

27. *Hook* : 3 ls x 3 eyed
    Whisks : Speckled grey mallard fibres
    Body : White floss, ribbed 4 turns black silk
    Hackle : Black and white speckled or grizzle cock

28. *Hook* : 3 ls x 2 up-eyed
    Whisks : 3 dark brown turkey feather fibres
    Tip : Black floss silk
    Body : White floss silk, ribbed 5 turns black floss silk
    Hackle : Ginger cock with grey speckled mallard breast over

29. *Hook* : 3 ls x 3 eyed
    Whisks : Brown speckled cock
    Body : Wheat straw, ribbed 3 turns red-brown silk
    Hackle : Cock, stained blue dun and light red cock

30. *Hook* : 3 ls x 3 eyed
    Whisks : Cock pheasant tail fibres
    Body : Primrose seal's fur ribbed 4 turns red-brown silk
    Hackle : Speckled grey mallard stained greenish and red cock

31. *Hook* : 3 ls x 2 eyed
    Whisks : Red-brown cock hackle fibres
    Body : Yellow seal's fur, ribbed 4 turns red-brown silk
    Hackle : Cock stained yellow

32. *Hook* : 4 down-eyed sneck bronzed
    Whisks : Cock golden pheasant tail fibres
    Butt : Bronze peacock herl
    Body : Bulky, olive seal's fur, ribbed 4 turns round gold tinsel

Hackle :	Ginger hen with well speckled woodcock hackle over
Head :	Peacock herl

Taken from *Modern Trout Fly Dressing*, the following are Roger Woolley's choice of hackled mayflies.

33. The Wood Duck

Body :	(1) Undyed raffia ribbed gold wire
	(2) undyed raffia-ribbed buff sewing silk
Tails :	Three strands cock pheasant tail feather
Hackles :	Ginger cock down body, wood duck at shoulder

34. The Colonel

Body :	Buff yellow floss silk ribbed gold wire
Tails :	Three strands cock pheasant tail feather
Hackles :	At shoulder only, the brown barred feather from flank of a partridge, intermingled with hen pheasant breast feather

Advice years earlier had included two other dressings:

35. The Parson

Body :	Yellowish lambs' wool with three ribs of peacock herl at tail end
Tails :	Three strands cock pheasant tail feather
Hackles :	Hen pheasant neck and wood duck hackles

36. The Frenchman
    Body :   Yellow dyed raffia
                  ribbed gold wire.
    Tails :   Three strands cock
                  pheasant tail feather
    Hackles :   Brassy dun down body,
                  barred French partridge
                  feather at shoulder

Woolley was of the opinion that the best hackled mayfly patterns were those tied with natural undyed feathers, but the following fly is close in dressing to the Frenchman:

37. *Hook* :   3 ls x 2 up-eyed
    Whisks :   3 cock pheasant tail fibres
    Body :   Yellow floss silk, palmered with light red cock hackle, ribbed 3
                  turns round gold tinsel
    Hackle :   Crimson stained cock with French partridge over

Butcher Mayflies

These dressings were written by Roger Woolley on the back of a slip of paper and tucked inside the back cover of his copy of *Modern Trout Fly Dressing*. The paper was a ticket from Tutbury gas works. None of the dressings in his fly-case are even close to these patterns. It would be of great interest to discover where Woolley obtained this information, since he obviously considered them to be of sufficient importance or interest to write them down and keep them in his book. There were no other dressings noted.

In 1963 Fosters of Ashbourne produced a booklet to celebrate their bicentenary. In this work, listed under 'Relics of the Past' is '1880 Butcher's fly book concerning the Derwent.' Roger Woolley would have certainly known W H Foster so perhaps the dressings came by that route. Fosters, too, thought the flies of interest, developing a 'Butcher Mayfly' series and illustrating a fly from this in their catalogue.

George Butcher was born in 1799 in, or near, the Derbyshire village of Calver. He made a

George Butcher's Light Butcher Mayfly with (previous page) Roger Woolley's dressing notes on the gas ticket found in his copy of *Modern Trout Fly Dressing*.

living on the Rivers Derwent and Wye acting as guide to both anglers and tourists visiting the locality. The mayfly patterns attributed to him are still used by anglers on Derbyshire rivers. Records in the Chatsworth Archive list the patterns in their monthly angling returns for the Derwent simply under the name 'Butcher'.

Their originator died in 1876 and is buried in Calver churchyard close to the Derwent banks. His headstone informs the world 'For many years of his life, amidst the beautiful works of God's creation, (he) followed as a fisherman the humble occupation of Christ's disciples.'

The patterns are as they appear on the reverse of the 'gas ticket', a receipt for gas supplied and dated April 2nd 1912.

38. Butcher Mayfly (Dark)
    Tail :   Red dyed fibres. Herl butt
    Body :   Red-orange seal's fur, ribbed gold. Ginger hen and olive dyed mallard hackles.
    Head :   Herl head

39. Butcher Mayfly (Light)
    Tail :   Mallard, herl butt
    Body :   Orange seal body
    Hackles: Same as previous fly just lighter.

The following fly is close in its dressing to the Light Butcher:

40.	*Hook* :	4 or 5 down-eyed sneck bronzed
	Whisks :	Speckled brown mallard or woodcock
	Butt :	Bronze peacock herl
	Body :	Orange seal's fur, ribbed 4 turns oval gold tinsel
	Hackle :	Ginger hen with brown and white speckled mallard or woodcock over
	Head :	Bronze peacock herl

A winged version of the 'Butcher' style dressings follows:

41.	*Hook* :	2 up-eyed 2 x ls bronzed
	Tail :	Golden pheasant tippet
	Butt :	Bronze peacock herl
	Body :	Scarlet floss silk with bronze peacock herl at the shoulder
	Hackle :	Dark brown cock tied full and bushy
	Wings :	Fan, grey-white duck breast or shoulder feathers

Loch Series

Loch patterns are mainly fancy flies designed to attract attention by colour and movement. Bright tinsel plays its part in this process, many of the waters in which these patterns are used are peat-stained.

The flies are known by the bird which provides the feather for the wing, allied with the colour of the body. Feathers from teal flank, woodcock wing, mallard bronze shoulder, grouse tail, jay wing, mallard blue, mallard white tip, bustard wing, cinnamon hen wing and hen pheasant wing may be used for the fly wings. Various colours of floss, silk fur and tinsels are used to create the bodies. Many of these dressings are listed in *Modern Trout Fly Dressing* but others are Roger Woolley's own variations on the theme. Hackles and tails are also varied – natural red for red bodies, ginger for yellow bodies and dyed blue materials for silver bodies, though this is by no means a hard and fast rule. Tail variations include golden pheasant tippets and toppings, red ibis, coloured wools and flosses.

White tipped mallard wing

This series is similar to the Heckham Peckham series credited to William Murdoch of Aberdeen. The blue feather from a mallard wing which has white tips is used to wing the following dressings:

1. *Hook* :   5 to gut, japanned
   Body :   Orange seal's fur, palmered red cock hackle, ribbed 5 turns gold oval
   Hackle :   Medium red cock
   Wing :   Mallard blue, white tipped

2. *Hook* :   5 to gut
   Tail :   Golden pheasant tippets ?
   Body :   Slate blue floss silk, ribbed 5 turns silver oval
   Hackle :   Black hen
   Wing :   Mallard blue, white tipped

3. *Hook* :   6 to gut, japanned
   Tail :   Golden pheasant tippets?
   Body :   Thin, black floss silk
   Hackle :   Black cock
   Wing :   Mallard blue, white tipped

4. *Hook* :   6 to gut, japanned
   Tail :   Grey speckled mallard fibres
   Body :   Primrose seal's fur, ribbed 5 turns oval silver tinsel
   Hackle :   Black hen
   Wing :   Mallard blue, white tipped

5. *Hook* :   6 to gut, japanned
   Tail :   Short, yellow wool
   Body :   Purple seal's fur, ribbed 4 turns flat gold tinsel
   Hackle :   Sparse, black cock
   Wing :   Mallard blue, white tipped

6.   *Hook* :   6 to gut, japanned
       Tail :   Red wool
       Body :   Amber seal's fur, ribbed 4 turns gold tinsel
       Hackle :   Medium red hen
       Wing :   Mallard blue, white-tipped

7.   *Hook* :   6 to gut, japanned
       Body :   Red seal's fur, ribbed 4 turns oval silver tinsel
       Hackle :   Black hen
       Wing :   Blue mallard, white tipped

8.   *Hook* :   6 to gut, japanned
       Body :   Brown silk or turkey fibre
       Hackle :   Dark red cock
       Wing :   Mallard blue, white tipped

9.   *Hook* :   7 to gut, japanned
       Tail :   Yellow wool
       Body :   Full, red seal's fur, ribbed 4 turns oval gold tinsel
       Hackle :   Black hen
       Wing :   Mallard blue, white tipped

10.   *Hook* :   7 to gut, japanned
       Tail :   Feather fibre stained orange
       Body :   Orange seal's fur, ribbed 4 turns oval gold tinsel
       Hackle :   Medium red hen
       Wing :   Mallard blue, white tipped

11.   *Hook* :   7 or 8 to gut, japanned
       Tail :   Long, golden pheasant tippets
       Body :   From tail, half yellow, half red seal's fur,
                  ribbed 5 turns flat gold tinsel
       Hackle :   Black hen
       Wing :   Blue mallard, white tipped

12. *Hook* : 7 to gut, japanned
    Silk : Black
    Tail : Red wool
    Body : Green Highlander seal's fur, ribbed 6 turns gold oval tinsel
    Hackle : Light red hen
    Wing : Blue mallard, white tipped

Bronze mallard wing

1. Mallard and Claret
   Hook : 4 to gut, blued
   Tail : Absent, possibly golden pheasant tippets
   Body : Claret floss silk, ribbed 6 turns gold wire
   Hackle : Black hen
   Wing : Bronze mallard fibres

2. In Roger Woolley & Co. fly packet as Lot's Fancy
   Hook : 4 down-eyed bronzed
   Tail : Black cock hackle fibres
   Body : Black seal's fur, ribbed 4 turns oval silver tinsel
   Hackle : Black cock
   Wing : Sooty black feather fibre, possibly crow secondary, paired with strip of red ibis or duck stained scarlet between

3. In Roger Woolley & Co. fly packet as Dark Mackerel
   Hook : 4 – 6 down-eyed bronzed
   Body : Claret floss silk, ribbed 5 turns round gold tinsel
   Body Hackle : Cock stained dark claret
   Wing : Dark bronze mallard fibres, full

4.   *Hook* :   4 to gut, japanned
     Tail :   Golden pheasant tippets
     Body :   Claret seal's fur, ribbed 5 turns oval gold tinsel
     Hackle :   Blue jay fibres
     Wing :   Probably bronze mallard, possibly hen pheasant tail fibres
                   (absent except stubs)

5.   *Hook* :   5 to gut, japanned
     Tail :   Bronze mallard fibres
     Body :   Orange seal's fur, ribbed 4 turns flat gold tinsel
     Hackle :   Black cock
     Wing :   Bronze mallard fibres

6.   *Hook* :   5 to gut, japanned
     Tip :   Silver wire
     Body :   Olive seal's fur, ribbed 6 turns silver wire
     Hackle :   Greenwell hen
     Wing :   Bronze mallard fibres

7.   Fiery Brown Variant
     Hook :   5 to gut, japanned
     Tip :   Oval gold tinsel
     Body :   Fiery-brown seal's fur,
                   ribbed 4 turns oval gold
                   tinsel
     Hackle :   Medium red hen
     Wing :   Rich, dark bronze mallard
                   fibres

8.   *Hook* :   5 to gut, japanned
     Body :   Dirty yellow seal's fur, ribbed 5 turns oval silver tinsel
     Hackle :   Medium red cock
     Wing :   Pale bronze mallard fibres
                   or brown speckled mallard breast fibres

9.   *Hook* :   5 to gut, japanned
      Body :   Orange floss silk, ribbed 5 turns oval gold tinsel
      Hackle :   Faded ginger or buff hen
      Wing :   Bronze mallard fibres

10.   *Hook* :   6 to gut, japanned
      Tag :   Oval gold tinsel, 2 or 3 turns wrapped on hook
      Tip :   White wool
      Body :   Crimson seal's fur, ribbed 5 turns oval silver tinsel
      Hackle :   Blue jay fibres
      Wing :   Pale bronze mallard or brown speckled feather fibres

11.   *Hook* :   6 to gut, japanned
      Tail :   Speckled brown mallard fibres
      Body :   Scarlet seal's fur, ribbed 4 turns flat gold tinsel
      Hackle :   Hen hackle stained scarlet
      Wing :   Bronze mallard fibres

12.   *Hook* :   6 to gut, japanned
      Body :   Claret seal's fur, heavily palmered with black cock hackle
      Front Hackle : As body
      Wing :   Bronze mallard, paired

13.   *Hook* :   6 to gut, japanned
      Tail :   Golden pheasant tippets
      Body :   Black seal's fur, ribbed 3 turns oval silver
      Thorax :   Yellow wool
      Wing :   Bronze mallard fibres

14.   *Hook* :   7 or 8 to gut, japanned
      Tail :   Speckled grey-brown mallard breast fibres
      Body :   Dirty yellow seal's fur, ribbed 4 turns double gold oval tinsel
      Hackle :   Brown speckled cock
      Wing :   Bronze mallard fibres

Grouse wing

1.   *Hook* :   5 to gut, japanned
       Tail :   Light red cock fibres
       Body :   Pale orange floss silk, ribbed 4 turns gold wire
       Hackle :   Speckled grouse
       Wing :   Mixed: grouse and cock pheasant tail fibres

2.   Grouse and Claret
       Hook :   5 to gut, japanned
       Tail :   Golden pheasant topping
       Body :   Claret seal's fur, ribbed 5 turns flat gold tinsel
       Hackle :   Grouse breast
       Wing :   Speckled grouse wing quill fibre, paired

3.   *Hook* :   5 to gut
       Tip :   Flat gold tinsel
       Tail :   Red ibis feather fibres
       Body :   Magenta wool, ribbed 4 turns flat gold tinsel
       Hackle :   Black cock
       Wing :   Dark grouse covert fibres

4.   *Hook* :   5 eyed
       Tail :   Light red cock hackle fibres
       Body :   Light olive seal's fur or wool, ribbed with the same shade of thread
               (Woolley often used waxed sewing thread for ribs and bodies.)
       Hackle :   Medium red cock
       Wing :   Starling or similar outer, grouse wing fibre inner *(This is an unusual wing construction but is very firm in texture and shape).*

5.   *Hook* :   6 to gut, japanned
       Tail :   Red cock hackle fibres
       Body :   Claret seal's fur, ribbed 4 turns flat gold tinsel
       Hackle :   Claret stained cock, bushy
       Wing :   Speckled grouse wing fibre, paired

6.   *Hook* :   7 to gut, japanned
       Body :   Magenta seal's fur, ribbed 6 turns flat gold tinsel
       Hackle :   Speckled grouse breast
       Wing :   Dark grouse tail or wing fibre, paired

Woodcock wing

1.   *Hook* :   3 to gut, japanned
       Whisks :   Primrose feather fibre, long
       Body :   Magenta seal's fur with palmered claret hackle, ribbed 4
                   turns flat gold tinsel
       Hackle :   Cock stained magenta
       Wing :   Woodcock or grouse feather fibre

2.   Hofland Fancy style
       Hook :   3 eyed
       Whisks :   Stained cock hackle fibres
       Body :   Claret seal's fur, ribbed 5 turns gold oval tinsel
       Hackle :   Cock stained claret
       Wing :   Woodcock wing quill

3.   In Roger Woolley & Co. fly packet as Malloch's Fly
       Hook :   4 down-eyed bronze
       Tip :   Gold floss silk
       Tail :   Red cock hackle fibres
       Body :   Cream lamb's wool ribbed 4 turns oval gold tinsel
       Body Hackle :   Ginger cock
       Wing :   Speckled woodcock or bronze mallard.

4.   *Hook* :   4 down-eyed bronze
       Tail :   Golden pheasant tippets
       Body :   Half natural seal's fur or lamb's wool, ribbed 4 turns fine gold
                   tinsel, half claret seal's fur left straggly
       Hackle :   Hen hackle stained royal blue
       Wing :   'Cloudy' woodcock wing quill fibre

5. *Hook* : 4 down-eyed bronze
    Tail : Red ibis, only stubs remain
    Body : Yellow seal's fur, ribbed 4 turns oval gold tinsel
    Hackle : Medium red hen
    Wing : Rich brown speckled woodcock or possibly mallard

6. *Hook* : 5 to gut, japanned
    Body : White floss silk, palmered with
    black cock hackle, ribbed 4
    turns flat gold tinsel
    Hackle : As body
    Wing : Woodcock wing quill fibre,
    paired

7. *Hook* : 6 to gut, japanned
    Whisks : Golden pheasant tippets
    Body : One third orange-brown seal's fur, two thirds claret seal's fur,
    ribbed 5 turns gold oval tinsel
    Hackle : Dark red cock
    Wing : Dark chestnut speckled fibres, woodcock or rich bronze mallard

Teal flank wing

1. *Hook* : 2 to gut, japanned
    Body : Peacock herl butt, white floss silk, peacock herl thorax
    Hackle : Light red cock
    Wing : Teal flank, paired, sparse

2. *Hook* : 2 to gut, japanned
    Body : Claret seal's fur, ribbed 4 turns oval gold tinsel
    Hackle : Black hen
    Wing : Teal flank, paired

3. *Hook* :   3 to gut, japanned
    Whisks :   Golden pheasant tippets
    Body :   Half amber seal's fur, half scarlet seal's fur; ribbed 3 turns flat
                 gold tinsel
    Hackle :   Light red cock
    Wing :   Teal flank fibres, sparse

4. *Hook* :   4 to gut, japanned
    Body :   Crimson seal's fur, bulky and carrot shaped
    Hackle :   Medium red cock
    Wing :   Teal flank fibres, dark

5. *Hook* :   4 ls x 2 to gut, japanned
    Body :   Amber lamb's wool
    Hackle :   Black hen
    Wing :   Teal flank fibres

6. *Hook* :   5 to gut, japanned
    Tail :   Bright yellow floss silk
                 or wool
    Body :   Bulky, one third scarlet
                 seal's fur, two thirds
                 black seal's fur; ribbed
                 oval silver tinsel
    Hackle :   Black hen
    Wing :   Teal flank, paired

7. *Hook* :   5 to gut, japanned
    Tail :   Yellow feather fibre
    Body :   Scarlet seal's fur, ribbed 5 turns flat gold tinsel
    Hackle :   Medium red cock
    Wing :   Pale teal flank fibres

8. *Hook* :   5 eyed, bronzed
    Tail :   Golden pheasant tippets

	Body :	Scarlet seal's fur, ribbed 4 turns flat gold tinsel
	Hackle :	Light red cock
	Wing :	Teal flank fibres, sparse

9.	*Hook* :	6 to gut, japanned
	Tail :	Red wool
	Body :	Yellow-olive seal's fur
	Hackle :	Absent
	Wing :	Teal flank fibres

10.	*Hook* :	6 to gut, japanned
	Whisks :	Dun cock hackle fibres
	Body :	Half white lamb's wool, half hare's ear fur; ribbed 7 turns oval gold tinsel
	Hackle :	Speckled brown partridge
	Wing :	Teal flank fibres

11.	*Hook* :	7 to gut, japanned
	Tag :	Flat gold tinsel
	Body :	Half yellow seal's fur, half turquoise seal's fur; ribbed 4 turns flat gold tinsel
	Hackle :	Black cock
	Wing :	Teal flank fibres, sparse

12.	*Hook* :	7 to gut, japanned
	Tail :	Speckled turkey fibres, dark
	Body :	Olive floss silk palmered with medium red cock hackle, ribbed 4 turns flat gold tinsel
	Hackle :	Medium red cock, bushy
	Wing :	Teal flank fibres

13.	*Hook* :	8 to gut, japanned
	Body :	Cream lamb's wool, ribbed 8 turns oval gold tinsel
	Hackle :	Probably light red cock, only stubs remain
	Wing :	Pale teal flank, sparse

14.   In Roger Woolley & Co. fly packet as Jungle Cock and Claret
      Hook :   4 down-eyedd bronze
      Tip :   Gold floss silk
      Tail :   Bronze mallard fibres
      Body :   Claret seal's fur, ribbed 5 turns fine oval gold tinsel
      Hackle :   Cock stained claret
      Wing :   Paired jungle cock feathers tied almost upright

Salmon, sea-trout and similar patterns

Many of the flies in this section have mixed wings, some of which incorporate married feather fibres of red, green, yellow or blue. Roger Woolley was considered to be a master in the building of married wings, a skill also acquired, via his tuition, by his daughters and employees. He advised the use of parrot feathers for these married strips although dyed swan or goose wing quill herl was also used. One client's assessment was, 'The married wings consisting of countless strands of exotic feathers were a joy to behold – never a fibre out of place.'

The 'Tag' described in the following patterns is the material wrapped nearest to the hook bend followed by the 'Tip', when two different materials are used, as shown in the diagrams from *500 Fly Dressings* by E Veniard. When a single material has been wrapped it is described as 'Tip' (the usual use of tag describes a short 'tail' on trout patterns).

The 'Tail' overlies both 'Tag' and 'Tip' followed by the 'Butt' which is wrapped over the tail root before the main body material.

Lighter dressed versions of these patterns on hooks 5, 6 or 7 would also be suitable for sea-trout according to Woolley's notes in *Modern Trout Fly Dressing*. He also says, 'The usual sea-trout fly is a dressing between the salmon and loch flies partaking of features of both these classes of flies.'

There are a number of large and somewhat simple patterns, which have a resemblance to low water flies, but are too bulky. Enquiries I have made about the dressings have resulted in little concrete information. Roger Woolley did tie salmon flies but generally only produced these to order and there are few patterns recorded in his writings. The flies in question would, no doubt, be suitable for a number of applications including river and loch fishing for salmon, sea-trout and large brown trout. It may be that these patterns are evolved from flies he came across during his time in Ireland and which he found successful, retaining them as a reference resource for future fly-dressing.

Most of these flies are tied to gut. Woolley's method of attaching this was used by many fly-dressers but may be of interest: A hook with a tapered shank was used and well-waxed silk wrapped tightly in open turns from half way down the shank to the shoulder. One end of the gut was flattened in the teeth, laid under the shank and lashed on with very tight turns of silk almost to the hook bend. A half hitch was made and the last three turns used to tie in tail, rib and body material. The silk was then returned to the shoulder in close touching turns and the hackle attached. The body, followed by the rib, was wound, the hackle wrapped and tied in and the wing fixed. A head was formed and finally varnished.

A further development was the dressing of midge doubles. Woolley says these flies were very popular but difficult to tie. One hook was tied to the gut, which was flattened and ridged – a second hook of exactly the same size then was tied alongside the first. The dressing was tied over both hooks and finished. In use the thumb nail was inserted between the hooks and they were opened to forty five degrees. The comment appended by Roger Woolley: 'Tying these midge doubles on gut will fully test your capabilities as a fly-dresser…'

Woolley's remarks on the use of flies to gut indicate that by the 1930s they were little-used though still had their enthusiasts. Some experienced flyfishers thought the flies dressed to gut swam and hooked better; others thought the security and convenience of eyed hooks preferable.

Mixed-wing flies

Woolley was keen to recommend mixed wings for both sea-trout and salmon patterns. He liked to use a fair amount of tinsel to create flash using size 2 to 4 hooks for low water flies and 5 to 7 for standard patterns.

1. *Hook* : 6 to gut, japanned
   Tip : White or faded gold floss silk
   Tail : Mixed, white, red, yellow feather fibre, brown speckled turkey
   Body : Blue seal's fur, ribbed 4 turns gold oval
   Hackle : Probably guinea fowl, (absent due to moth damage)
   Wing : Mixed: Golden pheasant tippet; married strands of red, blue, yellow, green fibre; guinea fowl fibres overall.
   Head : Black varnish

2. *Hook* : 8 to gut, japanned
   Tip : Oval silver tinsel
   Tail : Golden pheasant topping
   Body : Grass green seal's fur, ribbed 4 turns oval silver tinsel
   Hackle : Cock stained scarlet
   Wing : Mixed: golden pheasant tippet; married strands of white, red, blue fibre, speckled turkey, teal flank, blue macaw horns
   Head : Peacock herl

3. *Hook* : 8 gut-eyed, japanned
   Tip : Gold floss silk
   Tail : Mixed: teal flank; married strands of red and yellow fibre; golden pheasant tippet
   Body : Black seal's fur, ribbed 3 turns oval gold tinsel
   Hackle : Cock stained blue
   Wing : Mixed: Speckled brown turkey; golden pheasant tippet cheeks; married strands of red and yellow fibre overall
   Head : Peacock herl

4.   *Hook* :   6 to gut, japanned
        Tag :   Oval silver tinsel, 4 turns
        Tip :   Gold floss silk
        Tail :   Golden pheasant topping
        Body :   Black seal's fur, ribbed 4 turns oval silver tinsel
        Hackle :   Brown hen
        Wing :   Mixed: speckled brown turkey; married strands of red, yellow and green fibre, bronze mallard overall
        Head :   Black varnish

5.   *Hook* :   6 to gut, japanned
        Tag :   Oval silver tinsel
        Tip :   White floss silk
        Tail :   Mixed: married strands of blue, red and yellow fibre
        Body :   Claret seal's fur, ribbed 5 turns oval gold tinsel
        Hackle :   Furnace cock
        Wing :   Mixed: golden pheasant tippets; white goose or swan fibres, stained red goose fibre with possible golden pheasant topping overall

6.   *Hook* :   7 to gut, japanned
        Body :   Cinnamon seal's fur, ribbed 4 turns gold oval
        Hackle :   Cock stained yellow
        Wing :   Mixed: golden pheasant tippet, bronze mallard; peacock sword cheeks, red feather fibre with teal flank overall
        Head :   Black varnish

7.   *Hook* :   8 to gut, japanned
        Tail :   Golden pheasant tippets
        Body :   Half pale blue seal's fur, half orange seal's fur, ribbed 6 turns flat silver tinsel
        Hackle :   Blue jay and speckled partridge
        Wing :   Mixed: golden pheasant tippet with bronze mallard over
        Head :   Black varnish

8. *Hook* :   8 to gut, japanned
    Tail :   Speckled cock
    Body :   Red seal's fur, ribbed 4 turns flat gold tinsel
    Hackle :   Red cock and blue jay
    Wing :   Mixed: golden pheasant tippet
                  with brown speckled turkey overall
    Head :   Peacock herl

9. *Hook* :   9 to gut, japanned
    Tip :   Chestnut floss silk
    Tail: Golden pheasant topping
    Body :   Three quarters light blue seal's fur, one quarter red seal's fur,
                  ribbed 5 turns flat silver tinsel
    Hackle :   Sparse, grey hen
    Wing :   Mixed: bronze mallard;
                  strands of married red, yellow and blue fibre.
    Head :   Peacock herl

10. *Hook* :   8 gut-eyed, japanned
    Tag :   Oval silver tinsel, 4 turns
    Tail :   Bronze mallard
    Body :   Claret seal's fur, palmered with claret cock hackle
    Hackle :   Red cock
    Wing :   Mixed: dun feather fibre, golden pheasant tippet sides
                   - moth damage
    Head :   Peacock herl

11. *Hook* :   7 to gut, japanned
    Tag :   Flat silver tinsel
    Tip :   Blue floss silk
    Tail :   Golden pheasant topping
    Body :   Orange floss silk, ribbed 3 turns flat gold tinsel
    Hackle :   Speckled grouse, palmered
    Wing :   Mixed: bronze mallard; orange feather fibre overall
    Head :   Peacock herl

12.   *Hook* :   8 to gut, japanned
      Tip :   Gold floss silk
      Tail :   Golden pheasant topping
      Body :   Blue floss silk, palmered blue jay feather, ribbed 4 turns oval gold tinsel
      Hackle :   Scarlet dyed cock
      Wing :   Mixed: speckled brown turkey, scarlet feather fibre, golden pheasant tippet
      Head :   Peacock herl

13.   *Hook* :   8 to gut japanned
      Tail :   Golden pheasant topping
      Body :   Bulky, claret seal's fur, palmered claret cock, ribbed 4 turns oval gold tinsel
      Hackle :   Claret cock
      Wing :   Mixed: strands of red and yellow fibre, bronze mallard over
      Head :   Peacock herl

14.   *Hook* :   9 to gut, japanned
      Tip :   Oval gold tinsel, 3 turns
      Tail :   Red feather fibre and golden pheasant tippet
      Body :   Claret seal's fur, palmered claret cock hackle, ribbed 4 turns oval gold tinsel
      Hackle :   Claret cock
      Wing :   Mixed: golden pheasant tippet; dark speckled turkey or grouse overall

15.   *Hook* :   8 to gut, japanned
      Tail :   Golden pheasant topping
      Butt :   Peacock herl
      Body :   One quarter yellow floss silk, three quarters puce floss silk, ribbed 4 turns flat silver tinsel
      Hackle :   Spotted guinea fowl fibres and blue jay feather
      Wing :   Mixed: long brown speckled turkey fibres, golden pheasant toppings, blue macaw horns, feather fibre stained yellow
      Head :   Peacock herl

16.   *Hook* :   10 to gut, japanned
     Tag :   Flat silver tinsel
     Tail :   Golden pheasant topping
     Butt :   Peacock herl
     Body :   One third puce floss silk,
          two thirds yellow floss silk,
          ribbed 4 turns flat gold tinsel
Body Hackle : Sparse speckled mallard, probably stained olive-brown
     Hackle :   Blue jay
     Wing :   Mixed: long, speckled mallard stained light olive, golden
          pheasant toppings, blue macaw horns
     Head :   Peacock herl

17.   *Hook* :   9 to gut, japanned
     Tail :   Golden pheasant topping
     Body :   Fiery brown seal's fur,
          palmered red cock hackle,
          ribbed 6 turns oval gold tinsel
     Hackle :   Blue jay
     Wing :   Mixed: grey mallard wing
          quill fibres with teal flank overall

18.   *Hook* :   7 to gut, japanned
     Tail :   Grizzle cock fibres
     Body :   Amber seal's fur, ribbed 4 turns flat gold tinsel
     Hackle :   Cock stained claret
     Wing :   Mixed: grey mallard wing quill fibres with teal flank overall

19.   *Hook* :   5 to gut, japanned
     Tag :   Yellow silk or possibly gold oval
     Tip :   Crimson floss silk
     Tail :   Two cock hackle fibres stained bright red
     Body :   Black ostrich herl
     Hackle :   Long black hen
     Wing :   Mixed: pale grey mallard wing quill fibres with 2 fibres, stained
          red, married to upper edge

20.   *Hook* :   4 to gut, japanned
           Tail :   Golden pheasant tippets
           Body :   Claret seal's, palmered claret cock hackle,
                          ribbed 3 turns gold wire
           Hackle :   Blue jay
           Wing :   Mixed: bronze mallard; green feather fibre; golden pheasant
                          tippet sides

21.   *Hook* :   8 to gut, japanned
           Tip :   Yellow floss silk
           Tail :   Golden pheasant tippet
           Body :   Claret seal's fur, ribbed 4 turns flat gold tinsel
           Hackle :   Crimson dyed cock
           Wing :   Mixed: bronze mallard with green peacock sword cheeks

22.   *Hook* :   Bend to eye, 64 mm,
                          up-eyed, japanned
           Tag :   7 or 8 turns oval silver
                          tinsel

           Tip :   Primrose floss silk
           Tail :   Golden pheasant
                          toppings
           Body :   Primrose floss silk
           Body Hackle :   Kingfisher or kingfisher blue hackles
           Rib :   Black ostrich herl, 6 or 7 turns
           Front Hackle :   Gold cock
           Wing :   Mixed: golden pheasant tippets, 2 short, 2 long, chestnut saddle
                          hackle to tip of tail; kingfisher hackle and jungle cock cheeks,
                          golden pheasant topping overall
           Head :   Black varnish

23. *Hook* :   9 to gut, japanned
     Tag :   Gold oval tinsel
     Tail :   Married red and blue
                    macaw strands of feather
                    fibres
     Body :   Half yellow wool and half
                    red wool, ribbed 4 turns
                    oval gold tinsel
     Hackle :   Cock stained kingfisher
                    blue
     Wing :   Mixed: married blue, red and yellow fibre; teal flank and duck
                    egg blue feather fibre

24. *Hook* :   9 gut-eyed, japanned
     Tag :   7 turns oval silver tinsel
     Butt :   Black ostrich herl
     Tail :   Golden pheasant topping
     Body :   Flat silver tinsel
     Body Hackle : Possibly badger cock
     Rib :   Oval silver tinsel, 4 turns
     Front Hackle : Teal flank
     Wing :   Mixed: married strands blue, green and yellow fibre; strips of
                    teal flank, golden pheasant tail with bronze mallard over
     Head :   Black varnish

25. *Hook* :   9 down-eyed bronzed, also to gut, japanned
     Tag :   4 turns oval silver tinsel
     Tip :   Yellow floss silk
     Tail :   Golden pheasant topping
     Butt :   Red wool
     Body :   Medium blue floss silk
     Body Hackle : Cock stained light blue
     Rib :   Flat silver tinsel, 6 turns
     Front Hackle : Blue jay

Wing :   Mixed: married strands blue, red and yellow fibre, strips of teal flank and barred summer duck to sides, strips of bronze mallard and golden pheasant topping overall, 2 blue macaw horns

Head :   Red wool

26.   *Hook* :   8 down-eyed, japanned

     Tag :   Oval silver tinsel

     Tip :   Gold floss silk

     Tail :   Golden pheasant topping

     Butt :   Red wool

     Body :   Black ostrich herl

     Rib :   Oval silver tinsel, 4 turns

     Front Hackle : Guinea fowl fibres

     Wing :   Mixed: married strands of blue red and yellow fibre, speckled turkey fibres, golden pheasant tippet, jungle cock cheeks, golden pheasant topping overall, 2 blue macaw horns.

     Head :   Red wool, bulky

27.   *Hook* :   8 to gut, japanned

     Tag :   Oval silver tinsel

     Tip :   Primrose floss silk

     Tail :   Golden pheasant topping

     Body :   Black seal's fur, ribbed 4 turns oval silver tinsel

     Front Hackle : Dark blue dun hen

     Wing :   Mixed: married strands of green and red fibre, strips of pale speckled hen pheasant or golden pheasant tail fibres, bronze mallard overall

     Head :   Black varnish

28. *Hook* : 7 gut-eyed, japanned
Tag : Flat silver tinsel
Tail : Golden pheasant toppings, long
Butt : Red wool or seal's fur
Body : Sky blue wool or dubbing,
ribbed 5 turns oval silver tinsel
Front Hackle : Cock stained royal blue,
grey speckled mallard in front
Wing : Mixed: married strands of red, grey speckled and cinnamon
fibres, guinea fowl with two whole golden pheasant toppings
overall or as cheeks
Head : Black varnish

29. *Hook* : 8 gut-eyed
Tag : 8 to 10 turns fine oval
silver tinsel
Tail : Golden pheasant topping
Body : One third yellow floss
silk, two thirds black floss
silk, ribbed 4 turns oval
silver tinsel
Front Hackle : Probably guinea fowl but moth damaged
Wing : Mixed: full, speckled turkey, possibly grouse, long, teal flank,
married strands of yellow, red and blue fibre sides
Head : Black varnish, large

30. *Hook* : 7 eyed
Tag : Yellow floss silk
Tail : Golden pheasant tippets
Body : Claret seal's fur, ribbed 4 turns oval gold tinsel
Front Hackle : Cock stained light blue
Wing : Mixed: Golden pheasant tippet,
brown speckled turkey or mallard
Head : Black varnish

31.

Hook :	8 gut-eyed, japanned
Tip :	7 or 8 turns oval silver tinsel
Tail :	Golden pheasant tippets
Butt :	Red floss silk or wool
Body :	Flat silver, ribbed 5 turns oval silver tinsel
Front Hackle :	Claret, overlaid with light blue stained cock
Wing :	Mixed: married blue and red fibre, teal flank, speckled light bronze mallard overall
Head :	Black varnish, large

32.

Hook :	5 eyed, bronzed
Tag :	Oval silver tinsel, 2 turns
Tip :	Yellow floss silk
Tail :	Golden pheasant topping
Body :	Kingfisher blue floss silk
Body Hackle :	Cock stained kingfisher blue
Rib :	Oval silver tinsel, 4 turns
Front Hackle :	As body
Wing :	Mixed: golden pheasant tippet fibres, strips of red fibre, strips of golden pheasant tail fibre, bronze mallard overall
Head :	Black varnish

33.

Hook :	5 eyed, bronzed
Tail :	Golden pheasant topping
Body :	Flat gold tinsel, ribbed 5 turns stained orange cock hackle
Front Hackle :	Speckled grouse
Wing :	Speckled grouse with golden pheasant topping overall
Head :	Black varnish

34. *Hook* :   6 to gut, japanned
     Tail :   Golden pheasant tippets
     Body :   Black seal's fur
     Body Hackle : Cock stained magenta
     Rib :   4 turns oval gold tinsel
     Front Hackle : Cock stained kingfisher blue
     Wing :   Mixed: bronze mallard and golden pheasant tippets

Low water flies

Grey speckled mallard wing

1.   *Hook* :   8 to gut, japanned
     Tip :   Oval silver tinsel
     Body :   Half scarlet, half kingfisher blue seal's fur, ribbed 5 turns oval silver tinsel
     Wing :   Grey speckled mallard fibres tied flat
     Head :   Black varnish

2.   *Hook* :   8 to gut, japanned
     Tail :   Black whiskers
     Body :   Black floss silk, ribbed 5 turns silver wire
     Hackle :   Black cock
     Wing :   Grey speckled mallard fibres

3.   *Hook* :   9 to gut, japanned
     Tail :   Black and white teal flank fibres, sparse
     Body :   Scarlet wool, bulky, ribbed 4 turns flat gold tinsel
     Hackle :   Hen stained scarlet
     Wing :   Grey-brown speckled mallard fibres
     Head :   Black

4.   *Hook* :   10 to gut, japanned
     Tip :   Flat gold tinsel
     Tail :   Red feather fibre, long
     Body :   Green Highlander seal's fur, ribbed 6 turns flat gold tinsel
     Wing :   Grey speckled mallard breast, tied over the top of the fly

5. *Hook* :   9 to gut, japanned
    Tip :   Oval silver tinsel
    Tail :   Grey speckled mallard fibres
    Body :   Yellow floss silk, thin
    Body Hackle :   Palmered yellow cock
    Front Hackle : As body
    Wing :   Grey speckled mallard
    Head :   Black varnish

6. *Hook* :   9 to gut, japanned
    Body :   Half yellow-brown seal's fur, half fiery brown seal's fur, ribbed 5
                      turns flat gold tinsel, bulky
    Hackle :   Medium red cock
    Wing :   Grey-brown speckled mallard
    Head :   Black varnish

7. *Hook* :   7 to gut, japanned
    Tail :   Two fibres of scarlet feather fibre, very long
    Body :   Green Highlander floss or wool, ribbed 4 turns black thread
    Hackle :   Badger cock
    Wing :   Grey speckled mallard, sparse

8. *Hook* :   9 to gut, japanned
    Tip :   Oval gold tinsel, 4 turns
    Tail :   Mixed: golden pheasant tippets and teal flank fibres
    Body :   Grey lamb's wool, ribbed with doubled oval gold tinsel, 3 turns
    Hackle :   Blue dun hen
    Wing :   Grey-brown speckled mallard

9. *Hook* :   9 to gut, japanned
    Tail :   Yellow feather fibres
    Body :   Black seal's fur, picked out, ribbed 5 turns oval silver tinsel
    Wing :   Grey speckled mallard

10.   *Hook* :   10 to gut, japanned
      Tail :   Red feather fibres, very long
      Body :   Grass green wool or floss silk ribbed 6 turns flat gold tinsel
      Hackle :   Black with white tips, cock, long and bushy
      Wing :   Grey speckled mallard

Grey mallard quill winged

1.   *Hook* :   8 to gut, japanned
     Tag :   Oval gold tinsel, 3 turns
     Tip :   Puce floss silk
     Tail :   Golden pheasant topping
     Body :   One quarter yellow seal's fur, three quarters blue seal's fur, ribbed 5 turns oval gold tinsel
     Hackle :   Blue jay feather
     Wing :   Grey mallard wing quill fibre

2.   *Hook* :   0 to gut, japanned
     Tail :   Spotted guinea fowl fibres
     Body :   Yellow seal's fur, palmered medium red cock hackle
     Hackle :   Medium red cock
     Wing :   Grey mallard wing quill fibres

3.   *Hook* :   8 to gut , japanned
     Tag :   Oval silver tinsel
     Tip :   Yellow floss silk
     Body :   Dark blue seal's fur, ribbed medium oval silver tinsel
     Hackle :   Cock stained dark blue
     Wing :   Dark grey mallard wing quill fibre with two red horns overall

4.   *Hook* :   6 to gut, japanned
     Tag :   Oval silver tinsel, 4 turns
     Tip :   Claret floss silk
     Tail :   2 cock hackle fibres stained claret
     Body :   Black ostrich herl, bulky

Hackle :	Dark brown or black hen
Wing :	Grey mallard wing quill fibre with strand of orange fibre married to top edge, upright

Bronze mallard wing

1.
Hook :	5 to gut, japanned
Tag :	Oval gold tinsel, 2 turns
Tip :	Yellow floss silk
Tail :	Absent, possibly golden pheasant tippet fibres
Body :	Claret seal's fur
Body Hackle :	Cock stained claret
Rib :	Oval gold tinsel, 3 turns
Front Hackle :	As body
Wing :	Bronze mallard
Head :	Black varnish

2.
Hook :	6 to gut, japanned
Tip :	Blue floss silk
Tail :	Brown speckled fibres
Body :	Yellow-gold floss silk, palmered with a woodcock feather clipped back, the whole ribbed 5 turns oval silver tinsel
Hackle :	Woodcock covert
Wing :	Bronze mallard fibres
Head :	Dark peacock herl

3.
Hook :	6 to gut, japanned
Tag :	Oval gold tinsel
Tip :	Yellow floss silk
Body :	Claret seal's fur, ribbed 4 turns oval gold tinsel
Hackle :	Cock stained claret, full
Wing :	Bronze mallard fibres
Head :	Black varnish

4.   *Hook* :   7 to gut, japanned
   Tail :   Grey mallard fibres
   Body :   Cinnamon seal's fur, tapered, ribbed 5 or 6 turns yellow silk
   Hackle :   Buff cock
   Wing :   Bronze mallard fibres
   Head :   Black varnish

5.   *Hook* :   7 to gut, japanned
   Tip :   Flat gold tinsel
   Body :   Claret seal's fur, heavily palmered with a black cock hackle
   Front Hackle : Cock stained petrol blue, long
   Wing :   Bronze mallard fibres

6.   *Hook* :   8 to gut, japanned
   Body :   Green Highlander seal's fur
   Hackle :   Dark red cock
   Wing :   Dark and pale bronze mallard fibres

7.   *Hook* :   8 to gut, japanned
   Tag :   Flat gold tinsel
   Tip :   Orange floss silk
   Tail :   Golden pheasant tippets
   Body :   Claret seal's fur, ribbed 5 turns gold oval
   Hackle :   Hen stained claret
   Wing :   Bronze mallard fibres

8.   *Hook* :   8 to gut, japanned
   Tip :   Oval silver tinsel
   Tail :   Grizzle cock hackle fibres
   Body :   Petrol blue seal's fur, ribbed 6 turns oval silver tinsel
   Hackle :   Bushy black hen
   Wing :   Bronze mallard fibres
   Head :   Black varnish

9. *Hook* :   8 to gut, japanned
    Tag :   Oval gold tinsel
    Tip :   Orange floss silk
    Tail :   Golden pheasant topping
    Body :   Fiery-brown seal's fur, ribbed 4 turns gold wire
    Hackle :   Medium red cock
    Wing :   Dark bronze mallard fibres

10. *Hook* :   8 to gut, japanned
    Tip :   Oval gold tinsel
    Body :   Chrome yellow seal's fur, ribbed 5 turns oval gold tinsel
    Hackle :   Light red cock
    Wing :   Bronze mallard fibres

11. *Hook* :   9 gut-eyed
    Body :   Scarlet wool, ribbed 4 turns flat gold tinsel
    Hackle :   Black hen
    Wing :   Bronze mallard fibres
    Head :   Peacock herl

12. *Hook* :   9 gut-eyed
    Tail :   Golden pheasant tippet fibres, a good number
    Body :   Yellow floss silk, ribbed 4 turns silver wire
    Hackle :   Medium red cock
    Wing :   Dark and pale bronze mallard fibres
    Head :   Black varnish

13. *Hook* :   9 gut-eyed
    Tip :   Oval silver tinsel
    Tail :   Golden pheasant topping
    Body :   Orange-red seal's fur, ribbed 4 turns oval silver tinsel
    Front Hackle : Cock stained orange-red
    Wing :   Two pairs of bronze mallard
    Head :   Black varnish

14. *Hook* : 9 to gut, japanned
    Tail : Bronze mallard fibres
    Body : Green Highlander seal's fur, ribbed 5 turns gold tinsel
    Hackle : Cock stained green
    Wing : Bronze mallard, full
    Head : Black varnish

15. In Roger Woolley & Co., fly packet as Golden Emblem
    Hook : 9 down-eyed bronzed
    Tip : 4 turns gold oval tinsel, gold floss silk
    Body : Orange seal's fur, ribbed 6 turns oval gold tinsel
    Body Hackle : Cock stained orange
    Wing : Golden pheasant tippets with bronze mallard over
    Head : Black ostrich herl.

16. *Hook* : 9 to gut, japanned
    Body : Fiery-brown seal's fur, ribbed 4 turns oval gold tinsel
    Hackle : Medium red cock, long
    Wing : Bronze mallard, sparse

17. *Hook* : 10 to gut, japanned
    Tail : Brown speckled mallard fibres
    Body : Light olive seal's fur, heavily palmered with light red cock hackle
    Front Hackle : Medium red cock
    Wing : Upright bronze mallard fibres

18. *Hook* : 10 to gut, japanned
    Body : Amber seal's fur, ribbed 8 turns of yellow thread
    Hackle : Medium red cock
    Wing : Pale bronze mallard fibres

White duck 'satin' wing

1. *Hook* :   6 or 7 to gut, japanned
   Tail :   None
   Body :   Natural cream lambs' wool
   Hackle :   White cock
   Wing :   White duck wing quill fibre

2. *Hook* :   6 to gut, japanned
   Tip :   Flat gold tinsel
   Body :   Yellow seal's fur, ribbed 4 turns flat gold tinsel
   Hackle :   Cock, off white or slightly stained yellow, long

3. *Hook* :   7 gut-eyed, japanned
   Body :   Amber wool
   Hackle :   White cock
   Wing :   White duck wing quill fibre
   Head :   Black

4. *Hook* :   8 to gut, japanned
   Body :   White lambs' wool
   Hackle :   White cock
   Wing :   White duck wing quill fibre
   Head :   Light brown varnish
   Wing :   White duck wing quill fibre

Speckled turkey wing

1. *Hook* :   6 to gut, japanned
   Tail :   Long black and white speckled feather fibre
   Body :   Yellow-green seal's fur mixture
   Hackle :   Medium red cock, bushy
   Wing :   Brown speckled turkey fibre

2.   *Hook* :   8 down-eyed, x 2 long, bronzed
     Tail :   Ginger cock hackle
     fibres, full
     Body :   Ginger seal's fur, ribbed 5
                   to 6 turns oval gold tinsel
     Hackle :   Long, sparse ginger cock
     Wing :   Brown speckled turkey
                   feather fibre, possibly hen
                   pheasant wing fibre
     Head :   Black varnish

Pheasant tail wing

1.   *Hook* :   8 to gut, japanned
     Tag :   Yellow tying silk
     Tail :   Hen pheasant wing quill fibres
     Body :   Yellow-brown seal's fur, ribbed 4 turns yellow silk
     Wing :   Brown speckled hen pheasant or partridge fibres

2.   *Hook* :   9 to gut, japanned
     Tip :   Flat gold tinsel
     Body :   Yellow or gold floss silk, ribbed
                   4 turns ginger cock
     Front Hackle : Ginger cock, 2 turns, long
     Wing :   'Cloudy' hen pheasant or
                   woodcock wing quill fibre

3.   *Hook* :   9 to gut, japanned
     Tail :   Brown speckled turkey
     Body :   Grey feather fibre, ribbed 6 turns primrose floss silk
     Hackle :   Brown speckled turkey or brown speckled turkey
     Wing :   Hen pheasant tail fibres

4. *Hook* :   9 to gut, japanned
    Body :   Crimson wool, ribbed gold wire
    Hackle :   Buff hen
    Wing :   Hen pheasant wing quill fibre
    Head :   Black varnish

5. *Hook* :   10 gut-eyed, japanned
    Tag :   Flat gold tinsel
    Tail :   Long, strands bright red
                  feather fibre
    Body :   Dubbed hare body fur,
                  ribbed 5 turns flat gold tinsel
    Hackle :   Brown speckled turkey
    Wing :   Olive-brown hen

6. *Hook* :   10 gut-eyed, japanned
    Tail :   Golden pheasant tippets
    Body :   Electric blue floss silk, palmered with short fibred black hackle
    Wing :   Dark hen pheasant tail fibres

Teal flank wing

1. *Hook* :   10 to gut, japanned
    Tip :   Claret seal's fur
    Body :   Cream seal's fur, ribbed 4 turns flat gold tinsel
    Hackle :   Long medium red cock
    Wing :   Whole teal flank feathers
    Head :   Brown varnish

2. *Hook* :   10 to gut, japanned
    Body :   Green Highlander seal's fur,
                  ribbed 6 turns oval silver
                  or gold tinsel
    Hackle :   Cock stained green
    Wing :   Teal flank, full and large

3. *Hook* :   9 to gut, japanned
   Tail :   Red wool strands, sparse
   Body :   Pale yellow seal's fur, ribbed 4 turns flat silver tinsel
   Wing :   Teal flank, sparse

4. *Hook* :   9 to gut, japanned
   Tip :   Oval gold tinsel
   Body :   Orange seal's fur
   Hackle :   Light red or ginger cock, sparse
   Wing :   Teal flank, rolled
   Head :   Black varnish

5. *Hook* :   9 to gut, japanned
   Body :   Claret wool, ribbed 5 turns oval silver tinsel
   Hackle :   Badger hen
   Wing :   Teal flank

6. *Hook* :   9 to gut, japanned
   Tip :   Narrow flat gold tinsel
   Body :   Pale yellow seal's fur, ribbed 5 turns narrow flat gold tinsel
   Wing :   Teal flank

7. *Hook* :   9 to gut, japanned
   Tail :   Yellow wool
   Body :   From tail, one third red wool, two thirds green wool, ribbed 5 turns oval gold tinsel
   Hackle :   Light red cock
   Wing :   Teal flank, paired

8. *Hook* :   9 to gut, japanned
   Body :   Crimson seal's fur, ribbed 5 turns oval gold tinsel
   Hackle :   Light red cock
   Wing :   Teal flank feathers tied fan style as in a mayfly dressing.
   (Maybe intended as a dapping fly?)

9. *Hook* :   9 to gut, japanned
    Tip :   Oval silver tinsel, 2 turns
    Body :   Yellow-olive seal's fur mixture, ribbed 4 turns oval silver tinsel
    Hackle :   Black cock, long and sparse
    Wing :   Teal or wigeon flank, with a slightly brown cast, sparse.

10. *Hook* :   9 to gut, japanned
    Body :   Half crimson, half amber seal's fur, ribbed 4 turns medium flat
                  gold tinsel
    Hackle :   Light red cock, bulky
    Wing :   Teal flank

11. *Hook* :   8 to gut, japanned
    Body :   Yellow seal's fur, ribbed 4 turns flat gold tinsel
    Hackle :   Buff hen, sparse
    Wing :   Teal flank

A further leaf from Roger Woolley's flybook

CHAPTER THREE

Roger Woolley the Fly-dresser

Fly-dressers are copyists, and their task is to copy in form, size and colour, the natural flies and insects that form the main food of the trout and grayling of our streams — Modern Trout Fly Dressing

Roger Woolley's fly-dressing career began in a very different time to the present. Many anglers still fished with gut-eyed flies and flies dressed directly to lengths of horsehair or gut. A good many anglers believed that a fly to gut 'swam' better since it was in line with the draw of the cast. Eyed hooks had been available for thirty or forty years but were relatively slow to become popular, perhaps because of expense or simple prejudice. Woolley was still tying flies to gut - to order - in the 1930s and 1940s, but had been recommending eyed hooks since the 1920s. He requested anglers who required flies to gut to place their orders early as he did not hold stocks and dressed these patterns as required. Flies dressed on eyed hooks were stocked and packed in small folders or packets which bore the legend:

Trout and Grayling Flies
FROM
ROGER WOOLLEY,
Angler & Fly-dresser,
TUTBURY,
BURTON-ON-TRENT.

His specification of the ideal hook was stringent. Small smooth eye, good gape, small barb, smooth bends – not angular, and sharp points were his requirements. Nothing to argue with there, but hooks were a bone of contention among anglers. This is probably the reason a variety of hook styles are to be found among his flies. There would be little point in dressing flies on hooks his clients did not favour. In addition

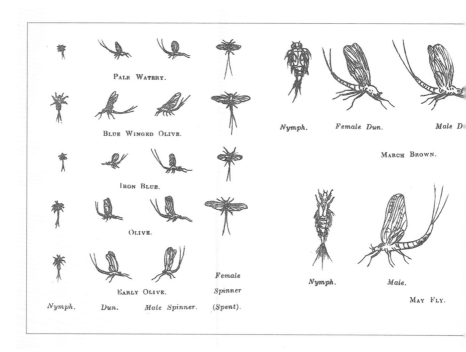

PALE WATERY.

BLUE WINGED OLIVE.

IRON BLUE.

OLIVE.

EARLY OLIVE.

Female Spinner (Spent).

Nymph. Dun. Male Spinner.

Nymph. Female Dun. Male Dun.

MARCH BROWN.

Nymph. Male.

MAY FLY.

Insect Identification Chart – fold-out from *Modern Trout Fly Dressing*

to this further limitations would be imposed by the range of hook currently available.

Woolley's advice to those who dress their own patterns was to strive for perfection in shade and form, keep an eye open to the potential of new materials and to be a 'copyist' of natural insects.

He was a self-taught entomologist and brought years of observation and study to bear on his fly-dressings. His aim was to copy, as accurately as possible, the natural insect his imitation represented. Although extremely knowledgeable Roger still captured insects to observe whilst tying. As a result, large numbers of his patterns are of his own invention and he recorded the dressings which were successful for both himself and clients. He was also an innovator, prepared to alter dressings if it was found to make the flies more effective. A gold tip added to the body of an olive or even the heretical suggestion of using stiff, bright cock hackles on North Country flies would have been extensively trialled by him, being found worthy of both comment and implementation.

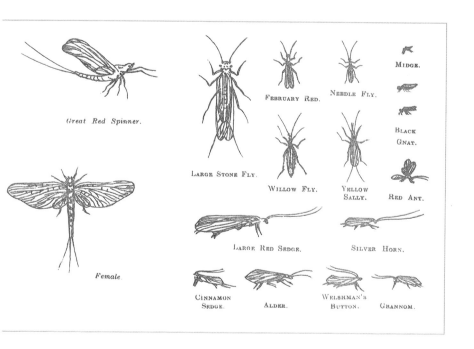

Great Red Spinner.

Large Stone Fly.

February Red.

Needle Fly.

Willow Fly.

Yellow Sally.

Midge.

Black Gnat.

Red Ant.

Large Red Sedge.

Silver Horn.

Female.

Cinnamon Sedge.

Alder.

Welshman's Button.

Grannom.

Famed as a grayling angler, he often used fancy flies of his own design, and within the collection are single pattern variations. These were not random dressings but the results of experience and experiment. Roger's Fancy, Grayling Steel Blue and Burton Blue developed from these origins. Among the many sea-trout, loch and wet flies in his fly-case are patterns which have gone unrecorded but which must be worth a 'swim' today.

The tools he used were few and simple: thin pointed scissors; another pair with curved blades which were seldom used; hackle pliers and a dubbing needle. In a photograph of Woolley at work there is also a pair of forceps to hand. He tied without the aid of a vice finding this gave a better feel for the materials and the fly being dressed. He also taught the same method to those who, years later, became his helpers or employees. Despite not using a vice himself, he mentions the Hawksley vice and also hand-vices for those who prefer the use of one. Having closely examined and attempted to tie some of his tiny midge patterns without a vice, I find the skill of Woolley and his team interesting. There is little evidence in photographs taken of them dressing flies with special lighting or any other aids to comfort. Relatives have told of how dark the workroom was; a table, chair, basic tools and materials being all that were needed.

Pearsall's Gossamer silk was his preferred tying thread; even in his time this was 'put up on convenient little reels'. Waxed silk was widely used not only to give colour but also shades to the dressings. Often the heads of smaller flies were not varnished and depended on a whip finish bonded with wax to secure the final turns of silk. If a dark wax was required the usual recourse was to the local cobbler for a piece of heelball which was used to polish shoe heels and welts. Colourless wax was mixed by the fly-tyer himself. Woolley favoured the recipe given by Francis Francis in *A Book on Angling*, 1867:

> Simmer two ounces of best resin with a quarter ounce of beeswax for ten minutes. Add a quarter ounce of tallow and continue simmering for a further fifteen minutes. Once the whole is melted pour it into cold water and work it with the fingers until soft and pliable. The more kneading it has the better it will be. If too hard, melt it and add more tallow, if it is too soft add extra resin. Methylated spirit is used to clean up afterwards.

Roger Woolley used different varnishes for different purposes: to varnish heads of flies he made up shellac varnish by placing the shellac in a bottle with methylated spirits and leaving until it had dissolved. The process was accelerated by shaking the bottle occasionally. A harder, penetrating varnish he made by dissolving old celluloid film in acetone. This was mixed thin to enable it to soak into the tying silk. Cellire, then manufactured on the Isle of Wight by Percy Wadham's Specialities Ltd., was used to varnish quill and raffia bodies to give strength. As today, it could be purchased in different colours for use on salmon and sea-trout patterns.

For material storage a cabinet with drawers or trays was used in addition to cigar boxes. These are, or were, made of aromatic cedar and as such repel insects. A further preventative device used by Roger Woolley to protect his stocks from moths was to make liberal use of 'Albo carbon,' (naphthalene?) going so far as to advise 'let your cabinet

Jack and Fred Woolley on the Mosley Estate, perhaps with fur and feather destined for Roger!

reek with its fumes', that would be really popular in many households today! Additional stocks of materials he stored in biscuit tins and boxes on the floor. On occasions when the River Dove entered the premises, family members were recruited to move everything above flood level.

His final ploy was to tempt the moths to warm, dark corners by providing boxes of useless fur and feathers in the hope the vermin would lay eggs there rather than on hard-won stock. Once the larvae hatched the whole lot was incinerated. It didn't always work – the edges of the felt leaves and a number of flies in his fly-case have been feasted on over the years. Without modern vacuum cleaners and compounds 'the moth' was a serious problem to clothes and fabrics in many homes, especially so in those of fly-dressers.

Sourcing materials for personal use would not be too difficult, but to obtain them in commercial quantity in the early days of his professional career may well have taxed Woolley's ingenuity. His need for materials could not be satisfied by surreptitious excursions into his wife's sewing basket, and the word was spread that Roger Woolley will 'give something' for suitable fur and feathers. Fellow tradesmen in Hatton and Tutbury would have been able to supply game-bird and poultry plumage, farmers and waggoners would find horsehair, rabbit, hare and mole pelts, not to mention the odd fox, otter and badger. These were supplemented by two of Roger's brothers, Jack and Fred, who were keen shots on the local Mosley Estate. However, being religious-minded, Roger was not too happy when in receipt of fur and feather procured on a Sunday.

Some of his favourite hackles were Grizzled, White and Blue Andalusian, but two capes he prized above all in good quality were Honey Dun and Brassy Dun. Both are very rare and Woolley regarded them as 'priceless'. There is the possibility he reared some of his own poultry but old cockerels no doubt came his way from a variety of sources; farms, smallholdings and back gardens. Whether he kept poultry or not he was an expert on when to cull birds for the highest quality hackles. Variables such as the age of the cock or hen, the exposure of the cape to summer sunlight together with the time of year were of considerable importance to the quality of capes.

A client who knew Woolley quoted, 'He seemed to have limitless supplies of magnificent cock hackles of the most delicate subtle shades and, as I remember, his flies sold at ridiculously cheap prices, 2/6d (12p) per dozen.' He added that Roger Woolley was a 'stickler' for being exactly correct in all aspects of his craft.

Allegedly, a wide selection of tying materials was provided by the 'Pegger's Men'. Around the turn of the 1900s a group of locals indulged in poaching around Tutbury and Hatton. Their base was the home of one of the gang who lived in Fishponds Lane which was known as the Pegger's Rest. The main quarry of the Pegger's Men were rabbits taken with a long let, 'peggers' being the men who positioned the hazel wands which supported the net. They viewed their activity as sporting rather than commercial, though excess conies were known to find their way to markets at Burton or Derby for 9d a brace. Neither Sir Oswald Mosley of Rolleston Hall nor the local constabulary shared the sporting views of the Peggers and quite possibly this added spice to their nocturnal excursions. It was said however, that the gang were never caught and the police sergeant seldom bought any meat! It was not unknown for the Pegger's Men to pursue other game than rabbits, the by-products of fur and feather would doubtless have been of considerable interest to any fly-dresser!

Local taxidermists often supplemented their income by the sale of fur and feathers, their off-cuts and parings would include some unusual materials; furriers workshops and slaughter-houses would also be frequented by those who plied the trade of Roger Woolley. In 1915 a hide and skin business was established by E. B. Chapman in the old corn mill in Tutbury. Beginning with horse slaughtering, this eventually became a tannery of all sorts of

E. B. Chapman working at the Cornmill Tanning Company he owned in Tutbury, also a likely source of fly-dressing materials for Roger Woolley.

skins, including calf, deer, sheep, goat, fox and badger. What better local resource could a fly-dresser desire?

The final recourse would be that of the fly-tyer's commercial supplier. Woolley was a perfectionist in his craft and well recognised the necessity of using the highest quality materials he could find to produce flies which would maintain and enhance his growing reputation.

In the absence of strong conservation laws, natural furs and feathers from rare and exotic creatures were legally available, though often at high prices. The supply of such materials was largely governed by the fashion for hats, boas and furs extant at the end of the nineteenth century. Those who could afford to buy such luxuries were certainly not short of money, and to satisfy this trade literally millions of birds and animals were killed worldwide over many decades and fly-dressers cannot be entirely exonerated from the slaughter. By the time Roger

Woolley's business was at its height the dotterel was a very rare bird in its mountain haunts, largely as a result of the demand for a North Country fly, the Dotterel Dun. Nor was this bird on its own – the supply of wood duck plumage for mayfly wings diminished leaving fly-dressers to devise ways of staining substitute feathers, and the decline of the corncrake had begun.

As Roger Woolley's reputation for quality fly-dressing and skilful angling grew, he began to deal and correspond with experts in both fields. Clients who required flies invented by these people would, no doubt, expect Woolley to provide appropriate patterns. Consequently he tied up samples and dispatched these to their originators, seeking advice and approval regarding production of the flies. It seems those contacted were suitably impressed and the initial request often resulted in high recommendations not only in the experts' own writings but also for publication by Roger Woolley in his catalogues. Further, regular correspondence began with, among others, G E M Skues, William Carter Platts and Richard Lake.

Woolley's catalogues advertise flies tied in the style of Harfield Edmonds and Norman Lee, Leonard West, General H C Eagles, J W Dunne, E M Tod, R C Bridgett; also G M La Branche and E R Hewitt, the then current experts on the 'new' method of salmon fishing with dry fly.

All these anglers provided Roger Woolley with patterns to copy and return for approval. Without exception he was permitted to dress and sell their fly patterns. General Henry Eagles, a well-known and successful angler on the Welsh border and Derbyshire rivers, sent precise angling notes with the patterns he provided, also supplying a list of his favoured sea-trout flies, again with notes which Woolley published in his catalogues.

Arthur Ransome specifically recommended Woolley's book *Modern Trout Fly Dressing* to anglers and fly-dressers. Skues went further, rating Woolley as one 'who has the somewhat exceptional qualification in his line of business of knowing something of anglers' entomology and of making a genuine endeavour to produce accurate representations of insects'. Skues also recognised that Woolley listed nymphs of Ephemerae but did not discuss either the methods of fishing them nor the ethics thereof.

Styles of winging flies

As a professional fly-tyer Woolley had his own methods and styles of dressing patterns, but also used what he considered to be the best of others. He was an advocate of the hackle-fibre wing as tied by John Henderson. This created a wing which gave the impression of translucency and also simulated the vein structure in a far more convincing manner than other styles of dressing – even when a fly was dressed sparsely with few fibres a good imitation resulted. The wing was very versatile – it could be tied spent, split, upright, dry or wet, enabling this method to be used for the wings of a broad spectrum of imitations, duns, spinners, alders and sedges, yet all would float reliably. Moreover the wing, once tied, always remained upright, flat or spent no matter what damage the fibres sustained. A sparse or bulky wing, according to need, was much easier to produce than with traditional methods of dressing. Depending on the number of hackle turns used and the fly being dressed, the wing could be light or heavy, transparent, opaque or 'glassy'. It overcame the great problems of fan mayfly wings: durability and buoyancy. The resultant flies also 'cocked' well on the water, something dear to the hearts of anglers in Woolley's time. Tied correctly, with top quality materials, the hackle-fibre wing was extremely strong and durable, and could be used until the fibres were literally worn away by the teeth of trout, torn away by the angler during unhooking or until it adorned a twig just out of reach.

John Henderson was an angler and fly-dresser of great experience. Like Roger Woolley, he applied considerable entomological knowledge to his fly patterns which were modelled on natural insects. A number of his articles written for the journal of The Flyfisher's Club were published in *Reservoir and Lake Flies* by John Veniard in 1970. Henderson fished at Blagdon reservoir in the early days of stillwater flyfishing and it is a possibility the Blagdon dressings advertised by Woolley were recommended to him by Henderson. Certainly Woolley listed both Henderson's dry flies for fishing lakes and rivers, advocating the use of Henderson's style of hackle-fibre wings for mayflies in his catalogues as early as 1919/20.

The wing is tied by catching the cock hackle in at the shoulder of the

BLUE DUN

MEDIUM
HONEY DUN

DARK
RUSTY DUN

SPANGLED
BLUE DUN

HONEY DUN

RUSTY DUN

DARK
RUSTY DUN

Roger Woolley's favoured dressing materials I

fly with two or three turns of silk. Several turns of silk are now wound to give a base for the wing. Up to six turns of hackle are made, depending on the density of wing required. The fibres of the hackle are parted with a dubbing needle and brought into the appropriate position for the pattern being tied. Using figure of eight lashings the wing is now fixed. For upright winged flies the fibres are fixed on top of the hook; for spent wings they are tied down underneath and on top, to make the fibres stand out horizontally at right angles to the hook. Turns of silk can be used to build up a thorax if required. Care is needed to manipulate the lashings in order to create the correct wing profile. Woolley notes that a bushy wing is neither necessary nor desirable, and thought two turns of hackle sufficient for the wings of dry fly spinners and duns, though more would be needed for mayfly wings.

Another associate of Roger Woolley, Reverend E S Daubeney, also developed a new method of dressing dry flies. Although these were not specific imitations of natural insects, Woolley was happy to advertise them in his later catalogues and to recommend them to anglers.

The body of the fly was minimal and the hackle palmered. Hackles used had to be of the highest quality, bright and stiff, to ensure the fly 'floated on its toes' and the hook remained well clear of the surface. This was intended to avoid the dense hook making a black shape on the water film. Hopefully, the impression created was that of a fly standing on the surface of the river. Good results were reported with dressings in the style of the Blue Winged Olive and of sedges, represented by a pattern which Daubeney christened the Mole Fly. Woolley felt the alder and mayfly could be adapted to this form of dressing and would prove 'irresistible'. These flies must be very similar to Baigent's Variants and to a Derbyshire pattern Woolley would have known well, the Kill Devil Spider.

Roger Woolley was very keen on both wet and dry hackled mayflies. He used natural undyed feathers as he thought these produced the best killing patterns. His favoured feathers were brown-barred partridge flank, hen pheasant breast, hen pheasant neck, wood duck, ginger cock, brassy dun cock and French partridge breast. He remarks on the new trend of adding an orange-red hackle to mayfly dressings without

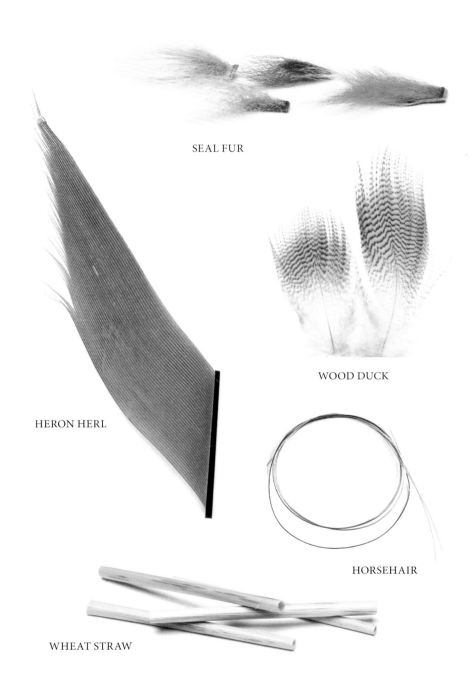

SEAL FUR

WOOD DUCK

HERON HERL

HORSEHAIR

WHEAT STRAW

Roger Woolley's favoured dressing materials II

further comment, though no flies in his case feature them.

He applied a great deal of effort in observing and researching mayfly nymphs' behaviour and working out appropriate patterns to imitate them. Now found in many anglers' fly boxes, the artificial nymph was uncommon in Woolley's time. He described the nymph as a 'meaty morsel'; careful observation had resulted in Roger noticing that prior to the nymphs hatching into duns, they were being actively hunted down by trout. As the nymphs ascended to the surface they were taken avidly and this was an opportunity or 'good bet' for the angler prepared to fish an imitation in an appropriate manner.

When dressing a mayfly nymph he stressed that the naturals are large, plump insects and accurate body size was of importance:

'A hackled Mayfly to imitate a hatching nymph is tied thus: Tie in a soft, short fibred hackle by the stem at the shoulder, tie in tails and ribbing wire, form body, wind hackle in even turns to half way down the body, keep in position by suspended hackle pliers, bring up ribbing wire and secure hackle with it, running the wire right through to the head of the fly. Tie in wire and finish off.'

This was 'a deadly form of fly to use' as mayflies began to hatch. His technique was to oil the fly and to cast it beyond a fish seen feeding on the ascending nymphs. The fly was then pulled under the surface, rising and lodging beneath the surface film as an emerger. As it drifted over the fish, it presented 'a very tempting morsel for any trout'.

There are several hackle point wing mayflies in Woolley's fly-case. He not only used hackle point wings on them but dressed spent spinners, long legged gnats and stoneflies in this style. For these smaller flies two hackle points were used, for mayflies four was normally the case. Natural feathers were often dyed by him to provide suitable colours and shades of wing. He appears to have had difficulty in sourcing natural cock hackles to meet his stringent standards for these patterns.

The hackles are tied on the hook back to back, separated and tied upright. They are then pressed flat and positioned by figure of eight lashings. In order to prevent the wing catching under the hook bend, sometimes a problem with this style of dressing, Woolley advised the hackle points used should be no longer than the hook shank from eye to bend.

By the time *Modern Trout Fly Dressing* was published in 1932, Roger Woolley had become disenchanted with fan-winged mayflies, saying they were outdated, easily damaged, difficult to present and prone to water-logging. A further observation was that 'discerning anglers', presumably his clients, were demanding a smaller mayfly imitation. It was found that these were no less successful than the larger bulky dressings. Nevertheless the majority of mayflies in his case are fan wings to gut, although it may well be that they have been retained to preserve successful or favourite patterns. For the sake of completion I include his opinions on the dressing of Fan Wings.

Suitable feathers for the wings are those from the breasts of mallard, wood duck, Egyptian goose, and teal. However Woolley's preference was for feathers from the outside of a Plymouth Rock cock wing. These are of a better shape and texture and the light coloured feathers could be dyed appropriate shades using natural or synthetic stains. The feathers were prepared by cutting off the unwanted herl. This left the herl stumps to provide a key on which the silk grips. They were then placed back to back and tied on the hook with several turns of silk. The stems were also bound together with alternate turns and using a figure of eight lashing, set as required.

In addition to those already discussed, Roger Woolley used the traditional styles of forming wings; for dry flies he lists single and double split wings for duns but also tied them 'pent' over the eye of the hook. When dressing sedges and alders the wing was laid back; for willow and needle flies it was tied tight to the back of the fly. For wet flies he used divided or rolled wings tied over the back, if necessary the rolled wing split in two by silk lashings. Many of the wet patterns contained in his fly-case have simple rolled wings, which can be easily dressed in an upright position.

The Glanrhos style of wet fly dressing was developed by L J Graham-Clarke a well-known angler on the Welsh border rivers and a member of The Flyfishers' Club. His contributions to *The Fishing Gazette* and other sporting journals were written under the nom de plume Glanrhos. He was at variance with several of his contemporaries of the time, favouring the wet fly. Graham-Clarke was interested in the fish's view of the fly and his style of dressing was used by Roger Woolley who valued this method for its 'brightness, action and movement of the fly in the water'. The wing is created by the tip of the hackle, the remainder being wound to imitate the legs. Obviously this limits the dressing to the imitation of insects whose wings and legs are of similar shades. With care the wing can be tied pent, upright or laid back to suit the pattern. The body is wrapped and the hackle prepared by stroking the fibres down, leaving sufficient tip for the size of wing required. Excess fibres at the base of the hackle shaft are removed to leave that required for the hackle which will represent the legs. The hackle is tied on the shank, the wing position adjusted and the hackle wound over the turns of silk that tie in the wing.

Though initially intended as wet fly dressings the patterns could also be used dry. In Woolley's opinion February Red, Needle Fly and Willow Fly were best tied using the Glanrhos style. This range of flies was advertised in early catalogues as 'Glanrhos's Amphibian Flies', presumably for their versatility and included a number of duns, March Browns and a Large Red Spinner. Roger Woolley considered the body of the latter pattern supplied by Leonard Graham-Clarke to be 'the prettiest body I have ever seen on a trout fly'.

Fly body styles

A number of flies in Roger Woolley's fly-case have bodies made from very different materials to those used now and some are constructed, in what may seem, novel ways. Fly-dressers are always experimenting with new and unusual materials and it was the same a hundred years ago. The popularity of dry fly angling fuelled the search for materials which would prolong the time a fly remained on the water surface. Fly floatants were limited in both effectiveness and availability. Woolley used a variety of materials and methods to make both wet and dry flies to suit his clients' foibles. In his writings he stressed the importance of the fly body, the most obvious part of the fly and the object of the fish's attack. It follows to make it as attractive as possible.

Roger Woolley's collection of body materials included many familiar to today's tyers, along with others long since discarded as 'new' products have become available. Pearsall's silk and floss in all colours, wools, seal's fur, mohair, raffia grass, quills, herls, horsehair, wheat straw, furs of many shades, flat gold and silver tinsel, gold and silver twist and oval, and gold and silver wire. In addition, skins of water vole, mole, rabbit, hare and if available, a heron body!

Some of his body constructions are very familiar, others less so:

Waxed tying silk body

The silk, of suitable colour, is caught on the hook one third of the distance between eye and bend. Wind it to the shoulder leaving a gap for the hackle, take the silk down the body in even turns, tying in whisks and ribbing as required. Return the silk to the shoulder taking care to wrap the turns closely and rib the body if needed.

Floss silk body

Catch the floss silk in at the shoulder of the fly and wind it down to the bend tying in the whisks, if needed. Return the floss to the shoulder in even turns, ensuring the body is flat and level.

(I have always been confused by the term peacock 'quill'. The material taken from the eye of the feather is, to my mind, 'herl'. That stripped from the feather shaft I would consider 'quill'. This may well muddy the waters still more.)

Peacock eye quill body (herl)

Remove a quill from the eye of a peacock tail feather. Strip the flue from the root end for about an inch and a half. The quill will have a light and dark stripe. For a dark body, tie in the quill on the off side of the hook with the lighter stripe uppermost. Conversely, if a lighter body is desired tie in the quill with the dark side upwards. Brown quill is obtained by stripping the flue from those down the sides of the tail feather. The quills are easier to use if they are dampened in warm water and kept in a damp cloth during tying. They can be made far more durable in use by the application of a coat of varnish after tying them in. Single colour quills which can be stained are to be found on the primaries of goose wings.

Feather shaft quill body

Different colours and shades of body material may be taken from the feather shafts of various birds. To remove the strip of quill, cut off the feather tip and tear away the quill downwards. If there is pith on the inner surface, scrape it off with a knife. For small flies the quill will need to be split down its length, for larger patterns such as sea-trout and salmon flies it can be used as it is. It can be stained different shades and is much easier to use when soaked. A good brown quill can be taken from the tail feather of a partridge and Woolley used the tail feather quill of the chaffinch for small black bodies. In these enlightened times, road kill, or a bird which has collided with a window may be the only source of chaffinch supply.

Celluloid body

Always keen to innovate and diversify, Roger Woolley must have pounced on old photograph film with delight. He washed it clean in soap and water, then cut it into strips 'similar to quill'. This was then wrapped over bodies of coloured silk or floss giving a delicate and natural result. Red Spinner, Apple Green Dun and Yellow Dun bodies were in his view, very suitable subjects for this treatment. Yet more realism was attempted by laying a darker shade of silk or floss along the top of the hook shank, a lighter shade along the bottom, securing both and covering with wraps of celluloid. This method is qualified by the proviso, 'I am not saying flies tied in this manner will kill any better than the normal patterns, but to those who like to be as exact as possible in every particular, this method will give pleasure.'

Gut and horsehair bodies

Both of these materials are best soaked before use. Catch in the whisks and gut or horsehair at the shoulder, wrap the gut or horsehair in touching turns to the tail tying in the whisks. If required the gut or horsehair can now be returned to the shoulder as a rib or solid body. Transparent horsehair will give a translucent body when dressed on a bare hook.

Dubbed body

Wind the silk to the hook bend tying in whisks and ribbing as needed. Wax the silk thoroughly and spin on the dubbing thinly and evenly. It is important to avoid lumpiness in the body. A second method is to catch the silk in at the shoulder, make a half hitch, wax the silk and apply the dubbing loosely. Wind the dubbed silk to the required body length, clean off the surplus dubbing and rib back to the shoulder in close turns. Woolley rated seal's fur above all other dubbing materials for the production of translucent bodies.

Roger Woolley does not seem to have been enamoured of detached bodies in any form. He precedes their dressing methods by remarking that whilst 'they look neat and natural … in practice they kill no better' continuing 'they are unnaturally stiff, and many anglers object to them on account of this stiffness'. Despite his objections there are various styles of detached body mayflies in his fly-case.

Detached body

The base of the body is either bristle or gut. Using waxed silk, tie in the appropriate body material and whisks on this base as on a normal hook. Make the body on the bristle or gut of the length required, and tie the body onto the hook. Continue to tie in the wings and hackle as usual to complete the fly.

Semi-detached body

The gut or bristle base is tied to the hook to a point half way down the hook shank. Whisks, body material and ribbing are now caught in on the gut or bristle base. The body is next made on the gut and hook shank, followed by wing and hackle. Woolley emphasises it is easy to make the body of an incorrect length, good judgement is necessary.

Semi-detached cork body

Tie in a gut or bristle base to the hook as before. Catch in the whisks and secure the silk at the tail end with a half hitch. Cut out of thin cork sheet an elongated cone shape with a blunt end. Form this carefully over both gut base and hook shank, securing with three or four turns of silk at the tail end. Rib the cork with the silk up to the shoulder and complete the fly.

Soft detached body

Oiled silk material is cut into a similar cone shape to the cork in the previous dressing. Cut a piece of white or yellow knitting wool and to this tie three cock pheasant tail fibres. Wrap the oiled silk cone over the wool base tying it tightly at the tail end and ribbing down the body formed with the silk. The body is now tied to the hook and the rest of the fly dressed. Woolley describes this style of body as '… juicy looking'.

Straw body

Several of the mayflies in Woolley's fly-case have straw bodies. In Modern Trout Fly Dressing he refers to wheat straw, presumably this was the most suitable type for fly-dressing. As far as I can ascertain, the straw was split and then cut to length prior to slipping it onto the hook shank. Thicker straw can be used by slicing it down its section. The material is much easier to use when slightly damp. The flies have a foundation of silk covering the hook shank which also ties in whisks when present. I believe the straw was placed over the silk base and tied down at the tail end with three or four turns of silk forming a butt. The silk was then ribbed up the body and varnished. On one pattern there are two ribs of different colours running next to one another. The straw varies in shade from fly to fly, but whether this is intentional or caused by ageing is difficult to say. Once the straw body is set in place the fly is finished off with wing and hackle as required.

Raffia body

Raffia of various shades is used as body material on the flies in the case. 'Natural' raffia is specified in some of Woolley's dressings, perhaps indicating that shade or colour differences were intentional and that the raffia had been stained. Raffia bodies once wound are ribbed with silk or floss, some being varnished.

Fly legs

Woolley says, 'From a fish's point of view the legs of a fly may not be very important, but to the dry flyfisherman the hackle used to imitate the legs of a dun or spinner is all important.'

He advised keeping the hackle as sparse as practicality permits since the natural fly has only six legs and it is the hackle which suggests these appendages. Further, an insect's legs are much the same length as its body and possibly need matching for colour too. Three 'rules' relating to hackles are given:

When fishing the wet fly upstream use a fly with soft hackles to create movement.

Use a wet fly with stiff hackles to fish down and across to prevent the hackle hiding the body when the fly is held against the current.

Dry flies need stiff hackles to help float the fly.

Woolley used standard methods to tie in hackles but on flies made for his own use sometimes, according to need, clipped the fibres short to stiffen them.

Winged or hackled wet fly

Take off the soft fibres of the hackle, tie in at the shoulder of the fly on the off side of the hook. The outside of the hackle should face the tyer. Remove the waste hackle stem and make the fly body. Wind the hackle on edge, tight up to the body with the required number of turns, tie off, and take the silk through the hackle to make the head or add the wing.

Palmer or Bumble

Strip off the flue from the hackle base. Hold the feather by the tip and stroke out all the fibres. According to the pattern, tie in at the tail or shoulder of the fly on the off side of the hook, with the outside of the feather once more facing the tyer. Make the body and wind the hackle through the body on edge. If the hackle is ribbed over each turn with fine wire, a far more durable fly results.

Winged dry fly

Prepare a stiff bright cock hackle, tie in on the off side of the hook with the inside of the hackle facing the tyer. When the hackle is wound it will have, 'an entirely different set' to that of the wet fly, and one, 'much to be preferred for dry flies'.

Dyeing and staining materials

Anglers and fly-dressers have long found the need to stain or dye materials to create the patterns they wish to use. Recipes exist in books and manuscripts going back centuries for wonderful concoctions which have been used to colour fur and feather; old natural stains were time-consuming to prepare, did not always give the same result but produced lovely subtle shades. Aniline and other chemical dyes developed in the nineteenth and twentieth centuries were easier to use, had more reliable results but tended to give hard glaring colours.

Roger Woolley's advice was simple: choose a cold winter's day on which to dye the materials in comfort and good light over a warm fire. Experiment and be prepared to learn from failure, often such failures result in a surprising and useful shade or colour. Take time to weigh out the ingredients accurately, mix carefully and record what has been done. Select feathers or furs which are of the same size and colour, as large pieces may well take dye differently to smaller ones. There is a tendency to use second-rate materials for dyeing – it is far better to use those of high quality. Any one batch may well vary with others so where a similar recipe has been used always process enough so it's consistent in colour. In *Modern Trout Fly Dressing* Woolley describes keeping a notebook in which he stuck samples of the furs and feathers he dyed. At the side of each are notes appertaining to the original colour and number of hackles, dye used, time left in dye, along with other details. His notebook obviously gave him great satisfaction: 'it will be wonderfully interesting and instructive to you and a source of pleasure to go through it occasionally'.

He gave no specific recipes of his own in *Modern Trout Fly Dressing* but includes details of those advocated by 'Ephemera' in *A Handbook of Angling* and F M Halford in *Floating Flies and How to Dress Them*.

As the fly-dressing side of Roger Woolley's business activity grew, demand outstripped his personal ability to produce flies for his clients so he trained his four daughters as fly-dressers, and possibly his wife too. It was Minnie, Roger's wife, who kept his business interests alive throughout his service in the First World War. By 1914 he was established as a fly-dresser so she would have been responsible to ensure supply of flies to clients over that period of time. Two of his daughters worked with their father in the business now called Roger Woolley & Co.

Rosa Smith and Audrey Leyland dressing flies

From the 1930s, more employees were taken on who worked for Roger over many years. Miss Rosa Smith, who was eventually to take over the business, was a fly-dresser for some thirty years, Mrs Audrey Leyland for about twenty five years, Miss Dorothy Fearn and Miss Vera Brassington for over ten years. These ladies tied flies without the use of a vice to the very exacting standards of their employer. Dressings deemed as below standard were returned to the workshop after inspection to be stripped, retied and steamed to pristine condition. As orders came in they were organised by Roger Woolley, required materials for the patterns ordered were packed into envelopes with transparent windows, and he then allocated them to the tyers' work tables. As the materials were processed into flies, these were placed back into the envelopes and sent back to Roger for packing, pricing and dispatch.

The fly-dressers worked without a vice

Rosa Smith with a fly storage drawer, also shown is the end of her work table

Fly storage drawer in Tutbury Museum. (Flies probably dressed by Rosa Smith.)

Roger Woolley worked both from his home and barber's shop in Marston Road, his tyers working in first floor rooms across the road . From these premises both wholesale and retail sales were made. The fly packets now had a different title and even a commercial motto:

Best flies kill most fish

get your

Trout and Grayling Flies

FROM

ROGER WOOLLEY & Co.,

Anglers and Flydressers,

Marston Road,

HATTON, DERBY

Regular orders came in from throughout the British Isles, Europe, America, India, Japan and New Zealand. His specialities were grayling and trout flies, though any pattern could be provided. Roger Woolley Mayflies were in considerable demand, perhaps as a result of his insistence of researching and adopting new patterns and dressing styles.

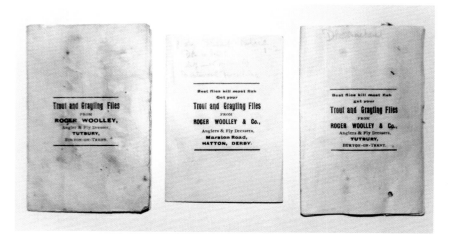

The detail on the fly packets alters with the development of the business. For much of his career Woolley worked from Marston Road in Hatton despite packets being annotated 'Tutbury'. The two towns are just the width of the Dove apart, the river forming the county boundary between Derbyshire and Staffordshire.

As a sideline, brooches dressed as salmon flies were also made and sold. Whilst the catalogues did not list large numbers of salmon patterns his reputation as a dresser of salmon and sea-trout flies continued to grow.

On 30 January 1948 a limited company, Roger Woolley and Co., Ltd., was established. The registered office was at Marston Road, complete with name-plate outside. Roger was managing director with his four daughters as co-directors. The company had a wide remit, presumably to facilitate possible development or expansion: 'Dressers, Manufacturers and Merchants of and Dealers in Flies, Hooks, Gaffs, Fishing Rods, Reels, Lines, Nets, Baskets, and all other Tackle' also offering expertise in practically every activity associated with angling, shooting and sporting requisites.

Roger Woolley readily embraced new developments in angling and fly-dressing: dry fly fishing for salmon, reservoir fishing for trout, orange hackled mayflies and alternative styles of winging all found places in his catalogues, writings or fly patterns. It can be said of him

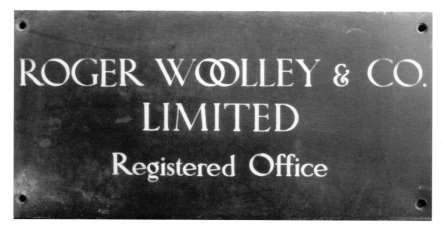

Business nameplate (now in Tutbury museum).

that he retained the best of the old and adopted the best of the new. He was rated by many as the best fly-dresser of his time.

Oakden's Claret and Tommy's Favourite

Woolley was the originator of many different fly patterns, usually copied from natural flies and using his own observations, but he also collaborated with others in their development. One of which was originated by his friend and sometime fishing partner, Major T H Oakden who lived near Hatton at Rolleston-on-Dove. This account of Oakden's Claret is taken from an unpublished manuscript by T K Wilson:

> 'This popular Midland pattern is one of the youngest of our fancies, and though a floater, it has a special attraction for nymphing trout; it is also a useful fly for grayling. It dates back to 1933, and was originated by Major T H Oakden, DSO, MC, RA, of Rolleston, Burton-on-Trent.
>
> The Major was flyfishing on the Dove one evening towards the end of June, and though there was a very good hatch of several varieties of duns, the trout refused all floating imitations, steadfastly continuing with their nymphing.

Oakden's Claret

Hook :   00 or 0

Body :   Crimson tying silk, well waxed

Hackle and tail : Dark blue dun cock's

Wings :   Hen blackbird or starling, tied as a single wing, and angled
to lean over the eye of the hook.

A dislike for nymph fishing at dusk set the unsuccessful angler pondering as to which artificial was most likely to tempt them to the surface. From experience The Major had learned that Dove trout preferred a pattern that was darker than the natural fly on the water, and they always came more readily at a slim-bodied creation that floated 'wing up'. A suggestion of red in the body was also considered a desirable feature.

The very next morning Major Oakden described to his friend Roger Woolley the fly he had in mind, and Woolley tied two or three specimens. He also suggested the name for the pattern and it was christened accordingly.

That evening, under conditions identical with those prevailing the previous evening, the new creation was tried and proved an immediate success, ten fine trout landed in two hours' fishing.

"Since then" writes Major Oakden, "it has been my principal stand-by, and from mid-May to August it has never let me down.

Tommy's Favourite as taken from *Modern Trout Fly Dressing*

Hook :	Sizes 00 – 1
Body :	Quill from a yellow-blue macaw tail feather, the yellow to show as body the blue flue as a rib
Tag :	Red floss, tip of silver tinsel under tag
Hackle :	Medium blue hen

I have also found it an excellent backend fly for grayling, and especially so when the olive dun is on the water."

And having found a winner, the Major went out of his way to ensure that other fishermen might share his discovery. He made a point of keeping a good stock of the fly in his case, and gave them to those of the fraternity he met on the river and who had failed to enjoy sport. Invariably they found the Claret successful, and as a result in a comparatively short time it was being used on many other English rivers besides the Dove.'

It is most deadly during warm weather, and when there is a hatch of duns it may be fished throughout the day.

On the Major's travels the fly accounted for trout and sea-trout from many different waters, even from French streams fishing with rudimentary tackle whilst he was on active service. The fish were a more than welcome supplement to the monotonous breakfast fare.'

Another fly developed by Roger Woolley was also involved in a day on the Okeover Club stretch of the River Dove with Major Oakden. At the invitation of Captain Okeover, via his waterkeeper Gregor Mackenzie, Woolley and Oakden were to fish the Okeover Club water to remove some of the grayling. Mackenzie, son of the Double Badger originator, reported on their visit in his book *Memoirs of a Ghillie*, 1978.

The anglers arrived on a sharp, frosty December morning and fished into the afternoon. Having completed his work the keeper walked up the river to find a heap of grayling, followed some distance later by another. He then met the anglers who were carrying still more fish. The catch was carried home, Mackenzie needing to return with a sack to complete the haul. Over tea Woolley and Oakden told the keeper there had been an all day hatch of winter duns and the two fly patterns they had used were the White Witch and a fly Woolley had tied up for Oakden and named, 'Tommy's Fancy' (or as it is recorded in *Modern Trout Fly Dressing*, 'Tommy's Favourite'). The river was fished upstream with the pair leapfrogging one another through the pools. The count for the day was 103 grayling, which were distributed by Gregor in the village the following day.

Many anglers on trout streams in the 1930s regarded grayling as vermin but, significantly, Gregor Mackenzie stresses how much Woolley and Oakden enjoyed the day and that some of 'his' members would have been amazed at such an attitude.

Philip Lupton, Harrogate-based angler and tackle dealer, designed 'Phil's Fancy' for use on the upper Nidd at Darley where he observed that the fish favoured species of fly with a steel-blue shade. Lupton was an official of the Harrogate Fly-Fishers' Club and long time friend of Roger Woolley, who dressed the pattern to the originator's instructions.

Much of my own angling is done on the Nidd and the pattern is as effective as ever on the water. T K Wilson, writing in Angling magazine, provides the details of this pattern:

Whisks :	Grey-blue hackle fibres
Body :	Grey Wool, ribbed with yellow silk
Hackle :	Blue dun cock
Head :	One turn of black peacock herl

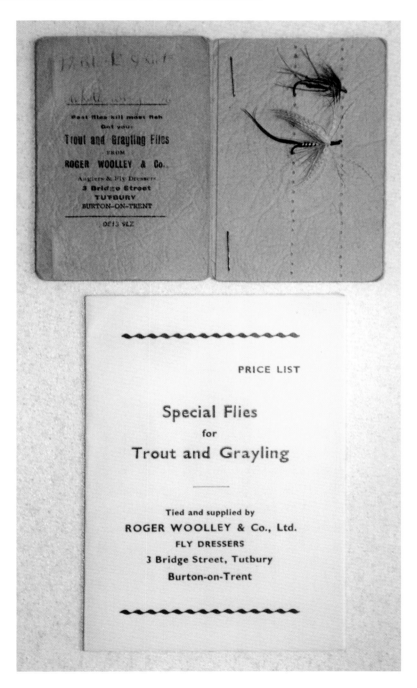

During the research for this work Noel Smith, who knew Roger Woolley well, referred to him as, 'a giant in his time' . When the business was wound up in the late 1950s Miss Rosa Smith bought it and continued to dress flies, under the title of:

ROGER WOOLLEY & Co., Ltd.
FLY-DRESSERS
3 Bridge Street, Tutbury
Burton-on-Trent

Rosa Smith produced a small price list under a similar title to Roger Woolley's, *Special Flies for Trout and Grayling*. Listed in the booklet of four pages are 39 different wet flies, nine grayling flies, nine nymphs, 30 dry flies, eight mayflies and 18 loch patterns with available hook sizes. The flies ranged in price from 8s to 10s per dozen. Clients' own patterns were supplied at a premium of 6d per dozen. Salmon patterns were available to special order, as was the fly renovation service previously offered by Roger Woolley himself. Local anglers were supplied direct, often waiting in the workshop for flies to be dressed. Flies were also sent to agents and tackle dealers countrywide, continuing with the service and network Roger Woolley had founded.

 Miss Smith continued to tie flies without resort to a vice as she had been taught, amazing clients with her expertise, particularly in the construction of complex salmon patterns. When she retired the company disappeared and according to local clients much of the stock and fittings were destroyed. Mr M A Smith who bought flies from Rosa Smith gave the following recollections of the business premises:

'The premises in Bridge Street, Tutbury, comprised of a terraced dwelling with no frontage in the way of a garden, the front door opened straight onto the pavement. On the front door was a brass plate with Woolley's name on it. On entering the premises

Opposite: Blue fly packet and catalogue as used by Rosa Smith after she acquired the business.

via the front door you entered a narrow hallway. On the left was an internal door which led to the room where Rosa worked. This room was at the front of the premises and had a large sliding sash window which gave good natural light to the room. The room was approximately 12ft x 15ft and had an open fireplace which was always lit as I recall. The walls were lined with full height veneer faced cabinets which had double doors. When opened these revealed drawers from top to bottom that were around two inches in depth. Each drawer had a series of circular recesses around four inches in diameter in which were contained flies of various sizes. You had to see it to believe it, there were literally thousands of flies in each cabinet. Presumably this was the stock that orders were picked from and then topped up again as they depleted.

The flies that I purchased were usually spider patterns and dry roof wing sedges (not dissimilar to Walker's Red Sedge pattern). I do not remember the exact price paid but it was no more than 20 pence per fly and they were purchased by the half dozen. If there were none in stock I would wait while Rosa tied them in a matter of minutes. As I recollect, the date would be around 1975 as this was when I first started flyfishing on the Dove.

The bench that Rosa worked at looked to me like a standard kitchen table and not something that had been specially constructed. There was a vice attached to it and a table lamp. I never saw the vice used although presumably it was or why would it be there? I witnessed Rosa tying flies on many occasions holding the hook in her left hand and the thread attached to a bobbin holder in her right. There were the standard array of tools on the table i.e. hackle pliers, dubbing needles and bobbin holders with various colours of thread.

Going back to the actual building, when viewed from the street it looked more like a house than a business premises. The door was on the right and the front window to the left had net curtains preventing anyone seeing inside. The woodwork was painted a dull orange colour. I do not remember the exact date when the premises closed but it must have been well before the 1980s.'

This was not the end of fly-dressing on the banks of the River Dove. In 1990 Derbyshire Fishing Flies was established in Hatton by Tim Thorpe – there must be something in the water around Hatton and Tutbury!

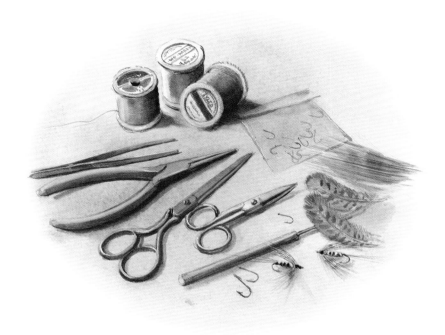

Dove tributary Sutton Brook, near Tutbury

CHAPTER FOUR

Roger Woolley the Angler

The flyfisherman with the greatest knowledge of natural and
artificial flies is in a position to obtain most sport
— Modern Trout Fly Dressing

Tutbury in Staffordshire and Hatton in Derbyshire are
separated by the width of the River Dove but joined by a
stone bridge which was rebuilt in the early nineteenth century. The river
forms the county boundaries for much of its length, and it has been the
haunt of anglers since the time of Izaak Walton and Charles Cotton.

Roger Woolley was born and brought up a very short distance from
the river in Tutbury on the Staffordshire bank. As a child he was attracted
to and fascinated by the river and its attendant wildlife, perhaps taking
family walks or playing along its banks; later paddling, swimming or
fishing with a cane, line, hook and worm. Whatever they were, the
nature of his early activities taught Roger to be an observant naturalist,
particularly interested in insect life associated with the river, not failing
to notice the dimples, swirls and strikes of fish feeding on the surface
nor their shadowy shapes hanging between the weed beds.

The River Dove during Roger Woolley's lifetime had its share of
pollution but generally speaking was prolific water, holding a good
variety of fish species. In 1861 the Commission for the Improvement of
Fisheries which was held at Burton-on-Trent reported that although the
establishment of mills had greatly diminished the salmon runs, there
was a good head of both trout and grayling in the river. This was some
years before Roger Woolley's birth but does give an indication of the
water's potential. Before the mill weirs were built the commission stated
migratory fish passed up river to Tutbury and Rocester. Older members
of Roger's immediate family may well have passed on anecdotes of
those times. His father was probably an angler and encouraged his son's
interest in fishing and in all matters piscatorial.

Roger made a close study of hatching insects, his enquiring mind leading him to identify the creatures both as nymphs and duns – an ability invaluable to any latent flyfisherman. Whilst still young he is said to have recorded his observations and findings in a series of notebooks which he added to throughout his life – information later put to good use in Roger's profession as a fly-dresser.

The River Dove fisheries around Tutbury were controlled by Sir Oswald Mosley of Rolleston Hall and a Mr Thornewell. They were well stocked and anglers fishing or dapping the fly would have been a common sight. Coarse fish also inhabited the waters and it seems probable that roach, chub, perch and barbel would be natural quarry after an apprenticeship of minnows and sticklebacks.

When the opportunity arose, Roger Woolley was an avid learner. His stay in Ireland was very influential regarding both fly-dressing and angling. In expert company he would have been able to absorb information and to learn new skills very rapidly, having little experience of either salmon or sea-trout angling, or familiarity with the waters in which they lived. On his return to England, he had built up a store of knowledge on which he drew for the rest of his life.

Back in Tutbury with his new wife, Minnie, he had to set about making a living for the family. Despite these commitments, he continued angling and fly-dressing.

His experience of local waters, the Dove, Churnet, Hamps, Blythe and Derwent, fished often at the invitation of owners or clients, coupled with visits to Yorkshire, Hampshire, Wales and Scotland over the ensuing years, resulted in a wide portfolio of angling experience. An example of this was a friendship and business association with Philip Lupton, an angler and tackle dealer from Harrogate. Roger Woolley dressed flies for Lupton, one in particular being named for him, 'Phil's Fancy'. The rivers Swale, Ure, Wharfe and Nidd became familiar waters to Woolley and he already had considerable knowledge of Irish rivers and loughs. He was, at some time, associated with Burton Mutual Anglers' Association as they sent a representative to attend Roger Woolley's funeral. As an angler and naturalist he deplored pollution in any form, being particularly vitriolic about the results of tar washings from the new Macadam road

Roger Woolley fishing the Dove

surfaces. Perhaps as a result of this, he became a member of the Anglers' Cooperative Association and was evangelical in his support. Raymond Hill, author of *Wings and Hackle* privately published in 1912 which deals with aspects of angling in Hampshire, Devon and Derbyshire, also stresses the pollution caused by tar washing from newly-surfaced roads. This must have been a bone of contention amongst anglers and naturalists throughout the country at the time.

The Mayfly, or Green Drake, fascinated Roger Woolley both as an insect and as an artificial fly. The period from mid-May to mid-June which covers the emerging and aerial activities of the species was evidently a time of intense observation over many decades for him. It was also the time he advised anglers to be on the river, from the hatching of nymphs to the end of the spinner fall, by so doing enabling them to make their own observations and conclusions. He also knew this was an opportunity to get on terms with the larger cannibal trout which sought more substantial prey than flies and their nymphs for much of the year. As an entomologist too, he no doubt anticipated the annual event with an open mind and considerable enthusiasm. After church on Sunday evenings, in the company of members of his family, he was to be found catching hatching insects. It may be these were caught to fish as live flies, or for sale as such, but Roger was still hunting them well into his seventies, most likely out of personal interest.

The reputation of 'Duffer's Fortnight' (as the period of the most prolific mayfly hatches is so quaintly but aptly known), did not always sit comfortably in Roger Woolley's mind. He thought a great deal of care was necessary to deceive the best fish, noticing their considerable caution or indifference at first, followed by increasing interest and confidence as the days of the hatch passed, ending with selective feeding latterly.

He continued his own personal research into natural flies, becoming one of the first angling writers to realise the importance of mayfly nymphs and emergers to anglers. In Roger's time these stages of the mayfly life cycle were largely ignored in favour of fishing the dun or spinner. He found fishing a nymph, wet or oiled, was often more successful in the period before the fish became conditioned to taking the surface fly.

His experience led him to conclude that mayfly nymphs attracted the attention of fish some seven to ten days prior to their hatching into duns. At that time, in the 1920s, mayfly nymphs were not often used by anglers. Perhaps this was due to 'the creed of the Dry Fly', lack of knowledge or anticipation of the imminent hatch. He remarked, 'There is much interesting work to be done before we find out exactly the information necessary, to enable anglers to know for certain just when, and how, to fish the nymph.' The method he found successful was to oil the fly, cast it upstream of a fish observed taking nymphs or emergers, pulling the fly under the surface and allowing it then to rise and enter the surface film. It was then allowed to drift over the quarry. Often trout would move 'up to a yard' to intercept the fly at any stage of the process.

His research into nymphs from different waters led him to deduce that the colour of the river substrate influenced that of nymphs living there. He also noticed, even in the same river, there were subtle differences of shade, depending on light or dark areas of the river bed. Artificial nymph patterns offered by Roger Woolley reflected these observations.

To deal with trout feeding on the emerging duns as they struggled from the nymphal shuck he dressed patterns which he called, 'semi-dry', stating that 'they kill well at times'. It now seems difficult to understand that anglers of Woolley's time largely ignored the potential of fishing artificials relating to these early stages of the mayfly hatch, particularly so in view of the then inherent difficulties of keeping flies afloat. A further example perhaps, of the 'Dry Fly' mind set.

He records the observations of Martin E Moseley from *Salmon & Trout* magazine written in June 1939. Moseley concluded that hatching nymphs could spend up to thirty minutes in the surface film before emerging as duns, and further, that they appeared silvery in appearance as air accumulated under the skin. Woolley stated his previous personal observations were probably flawed over the timing of the process and produced a series of 'Hatching Nymphs' using more gold or silver in the dressings and extra turns of hackle; the intention of the latter being to enable the oiled fly to be twitched under the surface, but then for it to rise under its own volition. He considered that these flies would meet the requirements of the dry fly fisherman.

Hackled mayfly patterns were among Roger Woolley's preferred flies. He used bright, stiff, cock hackles to tie his dry hackled mayflies, believing the trout like those patterns which 'stand up on their toes', an opinion he often quotes. Those he used to imitate the emerging dun, as wet or 'semi-dry' flies were dressed with soft hackles, particularly recommending the Parson, Colonel and Frenchman in these roles – 'no-one should be without these three patterns, for no more successful flies are tied.'

Later, in the light of Moseley's article, Woolley thought more silver in the dressings of his own hatching mayfly nymphs might increase their attraction to the trout.

As the duns hatch, develop, change into spinners, deposit eggs and die – 'the annual feast is on'. Although his earlier patterns had fan wings, latterly Woolley favoured John Henderson's method of dressing winged flies with bunched hackle fibres, giving the advantages of durability, buoyancy and the option of an upright or spent profile. Roger thought the spectacle of egg-laying and spinner fall to be a sight no angler would forget. He comments in his earlier catalogues of the growing trend for anglers to ask for smaller patterns and the fashion for a bright orange hackle to be included in mayfly dressings.

Grayling Witch

Flyfishing for grayling

Roger Woolley knew well the fickle ways of grayling, saying it was impossible to forecast the sport to come on any day or in any given conditions. For him, this very unpredictability probably offered the excitement and challenge he undoubtedly enjoyed so much, believing that to ensure both success and pleasure anglers should be familiar with the flies taken from the surface by the fish.

He thought August early enough in the season to begin flyfishing for grayling with dry fly; before this few good fish will be rising. September and October are the best months for using dry fly, though open weather in November will prolong sport, giving those fish still rising 'acquaintance with the inside of the creel'. Grayling are free rising to natural flies and imitations of olives and pale wateries, and Blue Winged Olives should be carried by the angler as both duns and spinners. Evening hatches of pale wateries can provoke considerable interest from grayling, as can the gold coloured spinners of the July dun. For cold days and later season duns and spinners of the Iron Blue will be required. Black gnats and long legged gnats are common over the water on warmer days, both being favourite prey of grayling – midges of various shades also featuring high on their diet. Woolley advised a selection of black, grey, green and badger dressed on tiny hooks (about half the size of a 000) – a number of these are present in one of Roger's fly-cases. The fish also feed on willow and needle flies, particularly under willow branches in the autumn, so imitations of these species will be useful.

Autopsies conducted by Richard Lake led him to conclude most of the graylings' feeding activity takes place beneath the surface, their food consisting of larvae, nymphs, shrimps, worms, terrestrials, dead and damaged flies. He also suggested that grayling, presumably along with other species, test or sample their prey items and this activity may account for their being deceived by artificial flies which bear little resemblance to real creatures.

Roger Woolley noticed when fishing for grayling on chalk streams he caught very few fish on dark coloured flies. The White Witch was his favoured pattern on these rivers; streams with darker gravelly beds required a darker pattern and here he used his beloved Grayling Steel Blue. His observation that it was the colour of the natural fly that was the clue to choosing the right artificial for grayling was no different from his previously-mentioned belief about following the natural colours of mayfly nymphs when tying artificials for trout.

He suggested that the angler should have a selection of wet hackle patterns for use when fish are feeding on nymphs; Waterhen Bloa, Greenwell Spider and Olive Bloa to imitate olives, the Poult Bloa for pale wateries, Dark Watchet for iron blue, Blue Hawk and Dark Needle to suggest needle and stoneflies and finally the Brown Owl as a willow fly imitation. Roger Woolley did not find sedges a success when fishing for grayling, saying that they did not rise well in the evenings. This is at some variance with remarks he makes about these flies in relation to trout fishing, thinking that sedges were much under-used by anglers. The Brown Owl is also used as a sedge imitation and no doubt grayling feed on sedge pupae as they ascend to emerge. He emphasised that often semi-submerged or low-riding flies were preferred and that they should not be over hackled. These flies were tied with long soft hackles to create movement, though on occasion Roger dressed them with stiff hackles for use in different conditions of water.

When no surface flies are being taken fancy dry flies can still be successful. The interest of grayling in bright flashy patterns was exploited most effectively by Roger when fishing both on and below the surface. On warm days he used small hooks, 00 and 000, increasing the size as the weather cooled and the season progressed. He says fancy flies work even when naturals are being taken, but on such occasions always found greater pleasure in fishing the imitation pattern. He thought there were few really good dry fly days, taking most of his fish on wet or fancy patterns. Whether or not this was the result of his preference for fishing in this style is impossible to say, but he discovered that by bringing wet flies carefully over rising fish grayling would take them well.

Richard Lake's observations of grayling feeding from the surface led him to conclude that as the fish take emerging or floating flies they 'bubble'. Whilst this phenomenon is not exclusive to grayling, Lake thought it an important identification feature of feeding grayling. This activity is also reported by Raymond Hill in *Wings and Hackle*.

Favourite fancy flies of Roger Woolley included Grayling Steel Blue, Grayling Witch, White Witch, Tommy's Favourite, Bradshaw's Fancy, Claret Bumble, MacKenzie's Fly and Red Tag. Around 1908 he devised a variant of his Grayling Witch nominating it as 'Roger's Fancy'. This pattern has tags of red floss at both head and tail, a heron herl body ribbed with flat silver tinsel and a pale blue hen hackle. Further variants of both these patterns had their tags wrapped on the hook. When fishing water with no fish showing, or on new water, his cast of the day always consisted of the Steel Blue and Grayling Witch. The group as a whole was also dual purpose, being fished wet or dry as circumstances dictated. In apparent contradiction of previous opinion, if these patterns failed to catch fish a poor day was to be expected!

Whilst on the subject of grayling flies, I have long been puzzled by the link between Roger and the 'Double Badger'. The pattern is often said to be the invention and a favourite of Woolley's, yet there is no mention of it in any of his publications – including the catalogues of flies.

In the course of my research Mr Noel Smith wrote to me and shed light on this conundrum. Herewith the relevant excerpt from his letter:

Donald MacLeahy MacKenzie on the Dove

'I first became fascinated with the art/craft of dry-fly fishing in 1937, when at the tender age of 13, I visited, for the first time, an aunt and uncle who, in retirement, had bought the local post-office and grocery store in Alstonefield on the border between Staffordshire and Derbyshire (the boundary being the beautiful, gin-clear limpid River Dove, full of gorgeous spotted trout!). Among the many pleasures I experienced was delivering the mail every morning, early, when I would deliver the letters to Dove Cottage, where lived a very famous character in the angling world – Mr Donald MacLeahy MacKenzie, keeper of the private stretch of trout fishing owned by the Manners family (i.e. the Duke of Rutland's family). It was he who first instructed me in the delicate art and craft of fly casting and introduced me to the now famous dry-fly, the Double Badger, which he himself had devised or 'invented'. At that time I was advised that, when my supplies of his Double Badger were used up/lost/worn-out etc, I should get in touch with a Mr Roger Woolley of Tutbury, Sudbury, Derby, (that was all – no phone number, no post-code in those days) to replace them. When in due course that time arrived, and I contacted Mr Woolley, by return of post I received a very conveniently illustrated pocket-book-sized, home-produced catalogue in black and white, listing every conceivable type of fly which Woolley dressed. Unbelievably, the Double Badger received no mention whatsoever, and he explained that he had never heard of it (although he gave the impression of being a personal friend of D M MacKenzie). I had to send my last extant copy of the fly so that he himself could make an exact copy of it and add it to his list of Derbyshire/Dove favourites!'

The Double Badger as dressed by Donald MacLeahy MacKenzie:

Hook : Down-eyed round bend or similar, sizes 14, 15, 16, 17 & 18.

Tying silk : Pearsall's Gossamer, black or purple.

Tail hackle : (Smaller than shoulder hackle) Early season – silver badger cock ; mid-summer to autumn – golden badger cock

Body : Bronze peacock herl, wound quite 'bushy'.

Shoulder as hackle : Slightly longer than the tail hackle, silver or golden badger cock, above (The hackles as taken from the cape should be an elongated oval shape, with a black root, gold or silver/white centre and a black list.)

'MacKenzie's Fly' referred to by Roger Woolley in the list of recommended dry patterns in Richard Lake's book *The Grayling*, is almost certainly the Double Badger.

On foggy October and November days Woolley advised the use of a good-sized Bumble, fished dry for rising fish. He was a great enthusiast of Derbyshire Bumbles for both trout and grayling fishing. These are versatile fancy patterns which can be used wet or dry, small or large. Roger Woolley's own Grayling Steel Blue is, to all intents, a bumble-style fly and one he fished, both wet or dry, according to the favour of the fish. Patterns Roger used and recommended in particular for grayling were: Claret, Mulberry, Rough and Light Bumbles, Grey Palmer, Blue Badger, Brunton's Fancy and Silver Twist.

As a result of his angling, fly-dressing and writing, Roger Woolley acquired a circle of influential angling associates. He knew, and

The Double Badger as dressed by Donald MacLeahy MacKenzie of Dove Cottage, Milldale. He was the probable originator of the pattern and the hackle shown is true to the style he used. MacKenzie and Woolley were friends and the latter refers to the 'MacKenzie Fly' in his notes written for *The Grayling* by Richard Lake. It is almost certain the two patterns are one and the same.

probably fished with, W H Foster of Ashbourne, William Carter Platts, G E M Skues, Arthur Ransome, his co-author of *The Grayling* Richard Lake and the Reverend E S Daubeney. A regular fishing partner was Major T H Oakden of Rolleston-on-Dove for whom Woolley named the two fly patterns Oakden's Claret and Tommy's Favourite. Several of these people deferred to Woolley in matters appertaining to grayling fishing, Skues commenting on his knowledge of entomology and skill at dressing artificial imitations. It may be that the fly in his fly-case labelled 'The Fisher for Windermere' was dressed for use by or at the request of Arthur Ransome.

In 1939 William Carter Platts wrote *Grayling Fishing* which included advice he had requested from Roger Woolley in order to clarify certain points. Some of Woolley's views may have been rather controversial at the time, particularly that of fishing downstream dry for grayling. Woolley had observed that grayling whilst apparently not being too concerned by the approach of a cautious angler were, on occasions, extremely tackle shy. In order to minimise the chances of the cast and line being seen by feeding fish he advocated casting downstream a yard above the surface, holding the cast in the air, pulling back and allowing it to fall lightly in front of the fish with about a yard of slack. The fly then drifts as naturally as possible over the fish. A fly presented in this manner, in Woolley's view, was more certain to be taken by the head-up style of rise typical of grayling. In order for this strategy to work wading is necessary to direct the fly. When fishing duns to rising fish Roger Woolley used a sparsely-dressed dry pattern with a single wing. If his downstream method was not practicable, he fished across and down with slack line to eliminate, as far as possible, any drag. He said grayling will come time and again at the fly. The fish rise freely to dry or wet fly and it is best to use small patterns in autumn, increasing the size of the flies through the winter. Although leaded fly patterns are commonplace today, Roger Woolley's advice to use integral weight to get the flies deep was quite unusual. He found a fly fished deep in the winter tended to catch the larger fish. When fishing flies beneath the surface he would always end the cast by a draw, followed by a strike, having found by experience the former often induced a fish to take without giving any indication.

Bait fishing for grayling

Whether or not grayling was Roger Woolley's favourite species, he was widely accepted as an expert grayling angler with both fly and bait. In fact, he seldom used bait, preferring to fish the fly except in water conditions when it was impracticable. He always said that if he had owned water only flyfishing would have been permitted. On the chalk streams he eschewed bait unless it was necessary to thin out stocks of fish. He recognised the method as a North Country tradition but thought it a sporting method only when using light tackle in conditions inappropriate for flyfishing; a smaller bag caught on fly was infinitely preferable to the large numbers of fish taken on bait.

He advised that grayling tackle should be fine and dainty and comprised of an eight or nine foot split cane rod, the action of which being 'stiffish but with an easy top'. The tip ring was lined and the intermediate rings of high bridge style to prevent, as far as possible, the line clinging to the rod. (This was a distinct tendency of the level silk lines used by coarse fishermen for much of Roger Woolley's lifetime as an angler.) He recommended a free running three-and-a-half inch centre-pin reel loaded with 40 or 50 yards of plaited silk line. The length of the line which came into contact with the water was well greased to ensure flotation.

Terminal tackle consisted of a quill or cork and quill float which would carry enough shot to allow the line to be trotted directly from the reel. A gut cast was tied to the end of the silk line, followed by a hook to gut completing the outfit. Care was needed when attaching the shot as nipping the gut could seriously weaken it. Hook sizes used were 12, 14 or 16, although it appears when dealing with bait fishing hooks, Roger referred to the old scale of sizing, rather than the new scale he lists for fly-dressings.

Whenever possible, he always advised the hunting angler to wade the river, believing this gave considerable advantages in searching every run, hole, riffle and pool. Added to this was much better control of the trotting tackle, and being lower in the water, the angler being less easily seen by his quarry. However, all of these factors are qualified by the importance of a quiet approach. Strangely, for a man so aware of the life of the river bed, he makes no comment on the effects of wading on plants and animals therein.

Attention has to be constantly given to the depth of the swims being fished, the tackle being adjusted accordingly. Indication of bites may be obvious or subtle. Any unusual activity of the float should meet with a response from the angler, being considered to be the interest of a taking fish. At the end of each trot through the swim the tackle should be held up, causing the bait to lift in the current. Woolley observed grayling often take at this point without the float giving any indication and consequently, he advised the angler to strike before retrieving the tackle.

The baits used by most grayling fishers in Woolley's time, as now, were worms or maggots, but he thought ground-baiting with maggots much overdone and unnecessary; a few baits trickled down the swim from time to time being all that was needed. He favoured the cockspur worm as a grayling bait, advising they be kept in moss for a few days to clean and toughen them.

Irish angling

Roger Woolley does not write in any great detail about angling in Ireland considering the influences his time there had upon his life's work as a fly-dresser and angler.

Such comment as is raised deals with the mayfly and sedges. On the loughs and rivers of Ireland, as elsewhere, mayfly fishing is the time to catch some of the larger fish which do not habitually take fly for much of the year – in Woolley's view particularly so on the loughs. He thought on these waters the strong winds and rough conditions required very buoyant flies, his hackle-fibre winged patterns being especially suitable both for surface fishing and dapping. Spent mayfly patterns dressed in a similar manner were especially deadly, of all flies Woolley considered the Spent Mayfly the best.

He found silver-horns to be common on Irish waters and particularly mentions an olive variety. These should be dressed sparsely for rivers and bushy for fishing the loughs. Black or Brown Silver-horns were, in Woolley's opinion, always worthwhile whenever the naturals were to be seen over the water, and particularly so where willow trees grew along the banks, the fly being fished close in beneath the trailing branches. Again the recommended pattern should be sparsely dressed after the style of Willow or Needle flies.

Roger Woolley on the river

Roger Woolley's fishing tackle has probably been long dispersed. Two items, the fly book and case (the inspirations for this book), certainly remain. The felt leaves of the fly book do not only contain flies. There are remnants of feathers and pieces of silk which although few in number now, point to the book containing fly-dressing materials for use at the waterside. When tying, Roger Woolley never used a vice so it would have been a simple matter for him to replace or tie new flies on the bank according to the requirements of the fish. There are also a number of photographs and from these I have devised a description of the tackle he used.

Woolley on the banks of the Dove

The rod in the photographs was split-cane, between eight and nine feet long, with a lined butt-ring placed quite close to the cigar-shaped handle. It had intermediate whippings, though was not close-whipped; the reel fitting is tight to the end of the rod, and appears to be screwed down the rod to attach the reel, which is of a relatively large diameter, probably plate faced. Dressed-silk lines were the norm and in his catalogues he advertises 'Red Loop' and 'Cormorant' gut casts, with or without droppers, and presumably he used these too. Certainly the advertisements rate these products highly, but then that is the nature of catalogues!

A substantial leather-bound fishing bag, of a flat box-like profile with a broad strap, is carried, these being the days when 'catch and release' was not widely practiced.

The landing net has a strong shaft of some four-and-a-half feet, a net ring of about 15 inches diameter carrying a deep knotted mesh net. The whole would also be suitable as a reliable wading aid. The net is suspended by Woolley's left hip, possibly by a cord across the shoulder and chest.

He is wearing rubber wading stockings or trousers. These appear to be of waist length and over them are lace-up wading boots. A tweed jacket, and cap into which are caught a number of flies, plus collar and tie completes the outfit.

Tutbury Bridge and the Dove

CHAPTER FIVE

Roger Woolley the Writer

These notes are written about the fly-fisher's flies from a fly-fisher's point of view only in the hope that they will greatly increase the interest, pleasure and sport of flyfishermen.

— The Fly-Fisher's Flies

Roger Woolley's formal schooling was probably complete by his early teens. Unless fortunate enough to gain a scholarship or be the offspring of wealthy parents, children left school at 13 or 14 in the late 19th century. This was less a reflection of the child's ability but more that of the society in which they lived. Any weekly contribution to the household budget was considered important, if not essential, by the parents of large families. Often the long term benefits of an extended education were ignored or simply not affordable.

Whilst at school, and after he left, Woolley allegedly filled exercise books with notes and sketches relating to his observations and activities at the waterside. T Donald Overfield reports on these records in *Famous Flies and their Originators* saying '…these show an intuitive ability to grasp the line and form of insects'. Bearing in mind Roger's early fascination with insects both in and out of the water, such records would be an invaluable resource and aid in his future career as fly-dresser and angler. It is possible that the simplified sketches which appear in *The Fly-Fisher's Flies* owe their origins to those made in his first records. The knowledge gained in youth via enthusiasm and observation formed a sound basis for future study and experience. The contents of these notebooks were probably Roger Woolley's first contributions to the pool of angling literature. They would be very interesting documents to read and to compare with his later writings but sadly I have not been able to find the originals.

Woolley's letters are penned in a neat, careful hand and contain concise detail. They are composed in a fluent and interesting style which can only have been acquired by practice. Whilst away serving in the

First World War he corresponded regularly with his family. He found time and space to discuss birds, plants and of course, fishing flies. Quite what the censor made of that would be interesting! Through his writing also comes evidence of his strong Christian faith and principles which were obviously of support to him whilst in Egypt.

Several of these letters were written with his children in mind. He made it clear that whilst he was unable to detail specific places and war activities he considered that observations of land, farming, village life and natural history may well have been of interest to those left at home. He reported on his journey through England by train to Birmingham then to Blackpool for training and finally embarkation for France, commenting on the numbers of cowslips on the railway embankments and the birds he saw on his journey.

His voyage to Le Havre was uneventful and there servicemen were put on the troop train bound for Marseilles. Roger was rather disappointed by what he saw of France though the extensive woodlands interested him, remarking that there were far fewer wild flowers and birds than at home, believing the cause of this to be the lack of hedgerows. He wrote of cows tethered in the fields on chains with people kneeling to milk them rather than using a milking stool as in England. Fields were large, but near villages and houses vegetable gardens covered every available piece of land. He saw many cherry orchards and on first sight thought the vineyards to be fields of runner beans. A good deal of space was given to descriptions of cultivation and pruning of the vines. He noticed an advertisement for Nestles milk and wondered if it had been canned in the dairy at Tutbury next to his home. The train journeys were long and uncomfortable and the men tired and very hot.

On arrival in Marseilles they joined men from France, America, Albania, Japan, China and the African colonies. The troopships were waiting and the servicemen marched in very hot and dusty conditions to embark. As ships filled up they drew offshore and anchored prior to forming their convoys, a process which took over two days, giving Roger time to describe the scenery and coast in detail. At this time the moon was full – 'night being like day with the light on the water.' He described the houses, hills and trees in a vivid manner before discussing the size of the ship … this by comparing it to the street where the children lived 'the deck is as long as from our house to Mrs ---- house'. Similar comparisons were made regarding the height and width of the vessel using the family garden and other familiar places around home.

On June 23rd 1918 they sailed for Egypt. The crossing of the Mediterranean was long and rough, again reported in relevant detail. Most people were ill and submarines were about, the convoy being escorted by Japanese battleships. On the way Roger observed a dove out of sight of land and as they drew close to port a hawk over the sea.

Disembarking at Kantara, they entrained for Ismalia. In the cities there were street traders of every description, ivory carvers receiving considerable attention in the letters. The rail journey was not pleasant. Temperatures of over 40°C ensured uniforms were drenched in sweat and men were packed into the carriages where they both ate and slept. However on this journey Roger Woolley describes an 'old friend' he met. The friend had a pretty, delicate body, large transparent wings and prominent gold eyes and was flying round an oil lamp. It was a golden eyed gauze wing, an insect he thought his daughters would recognise.

He saw hundreds of herons and storks on the banks of the Suez Canal and describes date palms, fig trees and melons as twice as big as footballs. Life size drawing of a large cockchafer and beetles are included in the text. The men went swimming in the Suez Canal, and in nearby public gardens prickly pears, date palms and pomegranates were growing. In the area near the hospital camp the population was extremely poor; their homes hovels, like pigsties. Roger writes of men sitting in groups smoking strange pipes with water containers through which the smoke is drawn and from his description he is obviously puzzled as to how the contraption works. The camp 'clock' was a hanging piece of railway track which was struck on the hour and half-hour by the guard on duty. Roger says this sounded exactly the same as the mill clock in Tutbury.

One of his letters outlines the differing customs of East and West. This includes examples of language with appropriate translations, and there are also details and discussions of comparative religion including a conversation Roger had with some Moslems, comparing Islam and Christianity. He hoped to go to Palestine in order to talk about the area to the Sunday school on his return home but whether he ever did is not recorded. A letter written in October 1918 gives some detail of his duties in the hospital; along with the supervision of local staff he administered medicine, took temperatures and nursed the ill and injured. There was a problem with fleas both for staff and patients. Woolley said 'they attack in close formation like the Germans used to do' and dealing with them was like 'rooting out the snipers'.

During the time Roger was away some of his children left school, and he reminds them all to practice their fly-dressing to make his job of training them easier on his return. He also asks the daughter responsible for the bookkeeping to keep him informed of how many flies are being sold and how the business is progressing, enquiring after his children's efforts in their various interests and exhorts them all to look after their mother.

Catalogues

Roger Woolley's first publications were almost certainly the catalogues of flies that he was offering for sale. These continued to be produced over several decades beginning in the early 1920s and became the foundations of his future articles and books. They were far more than simple fly lists with appended prices. Many tackle manufacturers advised on tackle and contemporary angling methods via their catalogues to their clients. Woolley adopted this approach, producing a document entitled *A List of Special and Grayling Flies for Dry*

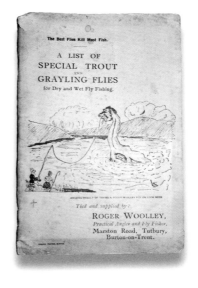

and Wet Fly Fishing, also bearing the legend '*The best Flies kill most Fish*', this slogan becoming part of the business's logo. Details on the cover are given as 'Roger Woolley, Practical Angler and Flyfisher, Marston Road, Tutbury, Burton-on-Trent'. Many years later when Roger Woolley

& Co. Ltd., was created this changed to 'Anglers and Fly-dressers, Marston Road, Hatton, Derby'. As Tutbury and Hatton are only the width of the River Dove apart it was perhaps only a matter of parochial loyalty as to which village Woolley chose for his address.

These booklets hold a wealth of relevant experience from a man considered by many to be an expert fly-dresser and angler. Much of the information found in the catalogues is mirrored in the two books he wrote but loses nothing for that.

The catalogues contain over 40 pages of fly dressings, advice and anecdotes, ending with letters received from satisfied clients each appended with the initials of the correspondent. It would be intriguing to discover the identities of Rev. F B H (Worksop), W S B (Church Stretton), C B C (Ludlow), A W P (Manchester), G A T (Yoxall, G W F (Gorseinon, S. Wales) J A L M H (Loughborough) W H (Northam, Devon) W T R (Leeds), Rev. R D R (Glamorgan), L T (Ashby), R C B (Herfordshire), H W B (Devonshire), H B C (Harrogate), W H (Bradford), J L N, A E H, R W D, E S A, A A, Col. R G M, F T, N H K (Col), F M D, F J S, C M T and J W J! Are the 'Great and the Good' of angling in Roger Woolley's time among them?

As the years passed, later versions contained new sections such as the fly patterns of the Rev. E S Daubeney. In these later copies, illustrations were also used in the form of photographs showing the styles of flies available. Included are black and white plates of

'Not only poaching but using Roger Wooley (sic) flies. Do you think I want my damn water skinned?'

dry flies for trout and grayling, patterns of G E M Skues, mayflies, wet flies and North Country patterns. The quality of reproduction is not good but they clearly convey the conformation of the various dressings.

In addition they also contained humorous cartoons extolling the virtues of Woolley's products. At least fourteen sketches were drawn up, nine of them being used in the catalogues. They were commissioned from artist L P Morinan, the earliest date on them being 1933, the latest 1936. (It is interesting that although 'Woolley' is spelt incorrectly 'Wooley' on the cartoons themselves, he did not insist on a correction before publication as he did with a similar error regarding the advertisements for the Rev. E S Daubeney's fly patterns.) One of the cartoons, showing a bank angler hooking the Loch Ness Monster, has been used as a catalogue cover. On this one the title has been typed and the spelling corrected.

They were signed in various styles over the years of production: L M, L P M, L Morinan and L P Morinan being appended at different times. Of the originals researched three are undated and one unsigned, some are drawn on watercolour paper, some on cartridge paper and all are in Indian ink. Various sizes of paper have been used, 7 by 7 inches, 7½ by 6 inches and 10 by 7 inches with some sheets having a cartoon on each side.

The tackle illustrated is of interest and it would appear that L P Morinan had rather more than a layman's knowledge of angling. Flyfishing, with Roger's flies of course, is portrayed as the most successful method of angling. Anglers with worm and float, spinning rod, centre-pin reel, minnow and gaff stand bemused by the success of a flyfisher using Woolley flies. Wading stockings, chest waders, plus-fours and brogues, tweed jackets and ties are all portrayed. In one cartoon there appears to be tools attached to the angler's jacket. The flyfishers wear hats festooned with flies, dressed by Roger Woolley of course. Some anglers carry their catch whilst others have a bag or creel. Two styles of net are shown, a wading net which can be slung across the shoulders and a 'flip-up' type attached to the creel strap. In the clubroom a line winder lies with a pile of tackle in the corner.

Inserts to the catalogues appeared from time to time, entitled *Up-to-Date Flies and Lightly Dressed Flies* which supported the advertised stock built up over the years. In earlier booklets these were in loose leaf form, later they became an integral part of the documents, part of the main text.

New patterns and angling developments were investigated by Woolley. These were then offered for sale (subject to his and their originators' approval) to clients. In these catalogues the number of well-known authors along with the associated styles of patterns, are witness to the respect the name of Roger Woolley engendered in angling circles.

Following pages : Four of the fourteen cartoons commissioned from L P Morinan for Woolley's catalogues.

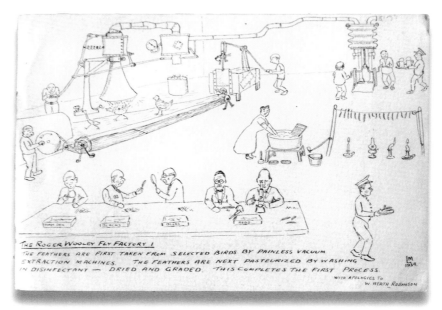

The Roger Woolley Fly Factory 1

Judge (summing up): 'I am determined this use of illegal baits shall cease. They are totally unnecessary. Roger Woolley's flies are as deadly as the best of them and strictly legal.'

Obtaining hackles for Roger Woolley

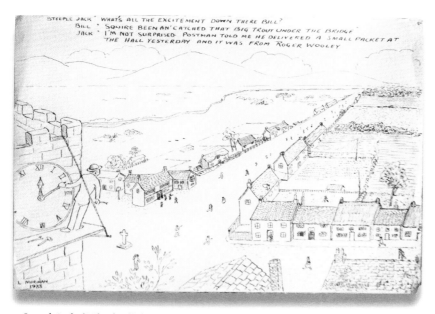

Steeplejack: 'What's all the excitement down there Bill?
Bill: 'Squire been and catched that big trout under the bridge'
Jack: ' I'm not surprised. Postman told me he delivered a small packet at the hall yesterday and it was from Roger Woolley.'

181

Licence to dress and sell the patterns of E M Tod, Edmonds and Lee, J W Dunne, F M Halford, Leonard West, General H C Eagles and R C Bridgett would not have been given lightly. Few other men, for example, were recommended in the writings of G E M Skues as entomologists and fly-dressers.

The price range of the flies offered obviously reflects the time involved in dressing and the quality of the materials used. All patterns except salmon flies were priced by the dozen. These are the pre-decimal mid 1920's prices.

Dry Flies	2/3d to 5/6d
Mayflies	3/6d to 5/6d
Wet Flies	2/3d to 3/6d
Reservoir Flies	4/- to 7/6d
Night Flies	10/6d to 15/-
Salmon Flies (each)	1/- to 1/3d (small) 1/9d (medium) 2/6d (large)

Catalogue contents

Dry flies

Roger Woolley was very careful of his reputation as a fly-dresser and stressed all his patterns were 'well and neatly tied with due regard to the size, shape and colour of the natural flies they are intended to imitate.'

Dry flies were available with double upright wings, rolled wings, hackle point wings and hackle-fibre wings. The former three styles were commonly used but the hackle-fibre wing, developed by John Henderson, really caught Woolley's eye. Prior to this development he thought the best of methods was that of using the wing feathers of various birds such as starling and blackbird. However, the hackle-fibre wing, when dressed with good materials, was in his opinion well worth any angler's trial from a number of standpoints – durability, buoyancy and versatility – and finally that of giving an excellent natural representation of the natural wing structure.

Spent spinners

A rise of fish caused by the fall of various spinners on warm afternoons, evenings and at dusk, demands the appropriate lightly dressed imitation and excellent presentation. As an aid to this Woolley recommended patterns lightly dressed with hackle-fibre wings. The cast was greased and the angler needed to be aware of the fly's exact position once cast on the water. As the spinners are low in the film, any interest shown by a target fish should result in a strike, although the fly itself may be unseen. Coupled with these recommendations is the proviso that the angler has some cognisance of the spinner species on the water. This is not easy fishing and Woolley points out that spinners are often neglected by anglers. However, when a fall is 'on' often no other method will enable fish to be caught. Woolley recommends that 'should fish be apparently rising at nothing' the appropriate spinner imitation of any duns which have been seen, may result in a successful outcome – the spinners being 'almost invisible to the naked eye' in the surface film.

J W Dunne's dry flies

Roger Woolley gives a brief account of Dunne's dressing method for his 'Sunshine Flies' and advises the angler to read Dunne's publication *Sunshine and the Dry Fly*. The method of dressing these patterns involved painting or enamelling the hook shank white and the use of cellulite artificial fibre for the body. As a result of this involved method, the price of these patterns was somewhat higher than normal. There followed a list of 42 patterns which Woolley would tie up as required.

Dry flies from the dressings of G E M Skues

Eighteen of Skues' patterns were offered for 'chalk streams and other difficult waters.' A number of these flies used rare hackles and supply depended on availability of the correct feathers – 'Mr Skues being rightly very insistent on the use of the correct hackles.' Woolley was in correspondence with Skues, who gives special mention of Woolley's skill as a fly-dresser and entomologist in *Nymph Fishing for Chalk Stream Trout*. He was evidently happy for the fly-tyer to advertise the patterns subject to specific dressing instructions.

Hackled dry flies

Not all anglers are expert casters and in dry fly angling good presentation is often the difference between success and failure. Great importance was given to the way in which a dry fly 'cocked' on the surface of the water in Roger Woolley's day. Less than expert casters often had trouble presenting the fly in this manner hence the popularisation of hackled dry flies. Roger used them himself and dressed some twenty different patterns for sale. 'Well tied hackle floaters will perhaps kill just as well as winged ones and are much easier to fish' was his advice.

Bearing in mind the contents of my own fly box and those of anglers I know, this is very true – hackled dry flies outnumbering winged patterns two to one, perhaps a reflection on my own casting abilities?

Palmer dry flies

Roger Woolley dressed a series of flies including March Browns, Blue Duns, Olives, Alders and Sedges with a palmered hackle. These he considered to be different to ordinary Palmer patterns. Their principal use was in conditions of rough water as they had far greater buoyancy than standard dry flies. The profile of the dun was lost, the compensation being ease of use in brooks and small hill rivers.

Long legged gnats

As their originator, Roger held great store by these flies for conditions of bright light and low water. He had observed them hovering over both still and running water in large clouds more often than most other species of insects – those which land or are blown onto the water eagerly taken by the fish. They are fished wet or dry and Woolley thought imitations in several colours should always be held handy. Gnats are lightly dressed and if winged, tied spent with hackle points and the hackle-fibre legs need to be twice the length of the body. There is a Gravel Bed fly and others in grey, brown, light olive, dark olive, yellow, green and ruby. The glassy glides inhabited by larger grayling are good places to use the Long Legged Gnat. Woolley informs his clients in a catalogue circa 1920 that his largest fly-caught trout succumbed to one of these patterns.

Midge duns, gnats and midges

These flies were specialities of Roger Woolley. The small fly box with his name inscribed contains examples of all three types and he recommended them for use in difficult weather on very clear, hard fished waters. The Derbyshire Dove, Wye and Derwent, his home rivers, are specifically mentioned in this respect. Midge duns were tied with an upright wing on tiny hooks being referred to as 'the cutest little flies made'. When using these patterns anglers were advised: 'they want fishing and fish need careful handling after hooking' and that they were 'very good for grayling'. Woolley's selection of gnats and midges were also suitable for similar conditions of weather and water.

Variants

Originally invented by Dr. Baigent of Northallerton, these patterns with their long bright cock hackles, are not unlike the Kill Devil Spiders used on the Derbyshire rivers. Roger Woolley tied them in the form of a lightly dressed dun and although being unsure as to the creature they were supposed to represent, likened them to small crane flies. He tied them up in a dozen different shades using high quality hackles to enable them to float very high on the water surface.

Rev. E S Daubeney's special dry flies

These patterns were given a high profile in some of the 1930s catalogues – a full page promotion being accorded to them. They formed another set of patterns similar in style to Baigent's Variants and Kill Devils. The originator and Woolley thought them to be made by an original and new method. The body was minimal and the whole fly stiffly hackled to ensure the bulk of the hook and shank was kept clear of the water – the object being to remove the outline of the metal hook. This is not dissimilar to the idea behind the dressings of J W Dunne, author of *Sunshine and the Dry Fly*. The impression created was, hopefully, to emulate a natural fly standing on the surface. Astonishing results were claimed for the flies; over a hundred brace of trout averaging one-and-a-half pounds were taken from a 'wild and difficult' Irish river by a party of anglers using these patterns. The flies were also found to be effective on the Test and Itchen where in all probability they were first developed.

Rev. Edmund Seymour Daubeney was born in 1868, son of Rev. Edmund Thomas Daubeney. From 1932-1947 he was Rector of Broughton near Stockbridge in Hampshire, quite close to the River Test. After leaving the rectory in 1947 he lived at 'Brooklyn', Broughton, Stockbridge, and survived into his early nineties.

There is a possibility that G E M Skues (who had given permission Woolley to produce and sell his own patterns) recommended Roger Woolley to E S Daubeney as an expert fly-dresser as their paths may have crossed when fishing on the Test and Itchen.

Roger Woolley was entrusted with the monopoly of dressing E S

Daubeney's four patterns in three sizes, large, medium and baby. The flies were known as: Red Robin (good on bright days), Black Robin, Blue Winged Olive (an excellent early season fly on Irish waters), Mole (a sedge style pattern which fished well in the evening or at night, particularly in Ireland.) In Woolley's opinion both the Alder and Mayfly tied in this way would make irresistible flies. The patterns were given considerable status by Roger in later catalogues but I can find no mention of them elsewhere. Perhaps even the reputation of Woolley was insufficient to propel them into general use.

Mayflies

A considerable amount of space is taken up with Woolley's comments on mayflies in his catalogues. To catch well, the angler needs to take advantage of all three stages of the fly; nymphs are attacked underwater, duns at the surface and spinners on or in the surface film. Despite the reputation of the mayfly season trout can be very fickle, much depending on prevailing conditions and the angler being present at the correct time with suitable imitations of the flies trout favour at that stage of the hatch. A strong recommendation is made by Roger Woolley for the hackle-fibre winged patterns, tied in the style of John Henderson, for both duns and spinners. Nevertheless, a range of pattern styles were offered along with the hackle-fibre winged flies which included ordinary mayflies, 'utility' mayflies, nymphs and floating hackled mayflies.

Floating hackled mayflies

These patterns were tied for those anglers who preferred a hackled mayfly (including Woolley himself). Using high quality cock hackles in their construction he produced buoyant flies which 'float like a thistle clock, and trout do like those patterns which stand up well on their toes.' He claimed them to be 'far in advance, in every way, to the usual soft feathered, gaudy dyed shop patterns.' Three specific patterns are advertised, perhaps particular favourites of Roger Woolley. The dressings of these patterns are taken from *Modern Trout Fly Dressing*. They are:

The 'Colonel' which was dressed with soft natural un-dyed hackles to suggest the mayfly as it emerges. It can be fished wet, emerging or dry with the advice that fish will come a yard to take it in. A subdued livery, combined with the way it is tied, are the factors in its success. The inventor of The Colonel is said to have had wonderful sport with the pattern on brooks and rivers wherever it was fished, and it is not unlikely the inventor was Roger Woolley himself.

Body :	Buff yellow floss silk ribbed gold wire
Tails :	Three strands cock pheasant tail fibre
Hackles :	At shoulder only; the barred brown feather from flank of a partridge, intermingled with hen pheasant breast feather

A smaller fly 'The Parson', again tied with subtle, natural shades of hackle, is described in Roger Woolley's quiet humour as 'just the chap to lead the trout in the way they should go.'

Body :	Yellowish lamb's wool with three ribs of peacock herl at tail end
Tails :	Three strands cock pheasant tail feather
Hackles :	Hen pheasant neck and wood duck hackles

A rather brighter and well-known fly, 'The Frenchman', completes the trio. The dressing of this fly also utilises only natural shades of hackle and was considered a deadly pattern.

Body :	Yellow dyed raffia ribbed gold wire.
Tails :	Three strands cock pheasant tail fibre
Hackles :	Brassy dun cock down body, barred French partridge feather at shoulder

Later catalogues include a fourth named fly in this section 'The Wood Duck'. The dressing for this fly is included with the other three in Modern Trout Fly Dressing and appears to be a later development.

Body :	(1) Undyed raffia ribbed gold wire
	(2) Undyed raffia ribbed buff sewing silk
Tails :	Three strands cock pheasant hackle fibre
Hackles :	Ginger cock down body, wood duck at shoulder

Woolley thought the mayfly body to be the most obvious target from the viewpoint of a hunting trout. He therefore dressed some 'Utility' mayfly patterns which incorporated bright, stiff and straggling game cock hackles which left the body exposed. These were tied wet or dry – 'Try them, you will find them good.' The difference in price between the various mayflies reflect the work involved and the quality of materials used. Both hackled floaters and hackle-fibre winged dressings are considerably dearer than 'Ordinary' and 'Utility' flies

Daddy Long Legs, Blue Dragon Fly and Yorkshire Stonefly

These rather odd bedfellows are grouped together as being 'useful for trout, on river and reservoir …on … hot windy days.' The Blue Dragon Fly is specified as a reservoir pattern, evidently being a damselfly imitation; the stonefly is described as the 'best pattern yet offered.' How well that remark went down in Yorkshire and North Country angling circles would be interesting! No other dressings of stoneflies appear in the catalogues, yet in later writings, Roger Woolley accords this group of insects considerable attention and importance, stressing they should be dressed thin and neatly on long shank 0 – 4 hooks.

Dry flies for salmon and sea-trout

At the time the first of Woolley's catalogues were penned, the use of dry flies when fishing for sea-trout and salmon was very new. He thought highly of the process of stalking and catching a salmon on dry fly and relished the 'pleasurable experimentation' necessary to sort out suitable and successful patterns. He throws in a stimulating mix of ideas for research: natural, sober colours; brighter traditional salmon fly shades; sizes of dressings; certain colours for specific rivers all being put forward as suggestions for trial. Roger tied up selections of experimental flies, adding that the results would interest him as much as his clients.

George La Branche was an American angler with a great interest in fishing the dry fly. He wrote *The Dry Fly in Fast Water* and *The Salmon and the Dry Fly* in the 1920s. Another American, Edward R Hewitt, was a well-known angler and successful author. He was a wealthy man and fished throughout U S A, Canada and Europe. His publications included *Secrets of the Salmon* (1922), *Telling on the Trout* (1926), Hewitt's *Handbook of Flyfishing* (1933) and *A Trout and Salmon Fisherman for Seventy Five Years* (1948).

These authors were both pioneers in the relatively new practice of fishing with dry flies for salmon and Woolley made sure that he was able to supply the patterns they recommended. He assured clients the flies would be dressed 'using only the brightest and stiffest of hackles, so that flies float well up on their toes.'

Dry fly patterns for sea-trout were confined to trout flies dressed on larger hooks, using 3, 4 and 5 new scale. Flies named are Sedges, Wickham's Fancy, Alder and March Brown along with 'several good Palmers'. Roger would produce any other fancy patterns requested by clients.

At the end of this section is a telling statement with regard to Roger Woolley's confidence in the quality of his product. He offers accurately tied dressings of any dry flies described by the authorities of the time: F M Halford, G E M Skues, Leonard West and for the Scottish rivers, R C Bridgett – a bold claim and heavy responsibility for any fly-dresser.

Wet flies

During the period when Roger Woolley was learning his craft and building up his business wet fly fishing was taking a back seat in favour of dry fly. He bemoans the fact that improvements in fly-dressing over this time were principally in the field of the dry fly and that wet flies were still dressed in the same manner as they were 50 years ago. Continuing to develop his theme, he says that in some areas 'the younger generation of flyfishers are very indifferent performers with the wet fly' having embraced the new faith (of the dry fly) and consequently neglected an important facet of their 'angling education'. Woolley certainly considered this a serious mistake and was not afraid to publicise his opinion; his view being that an open mind and the use of a variety of methods were more likely to result in sport on any given day.

He adapted John Henderson's hackle-fibre wing to the dressing of wet flies. This resulted in flies which were better in shape, lighter in dressing and altogether more delicate whilst being durable. The method also enabled him to tie flies to exactly the style requested by customers, even using bright cock hackles for wet patterns as were then in use by professional anglers on the continent. Roger's business interests had made him aware of the fact that in France, Corsica and Spain, for instance, ordinary English wet flies were considered to be quite useless. Traditional British anglers preferred soft hackled flies and Woolley thought the hackle-fibre wing both suitable for, and superior to, older dressing styles. Standard wet fly patterns were offered with the option that any others could be dressed to order.

G E M Skues winged wet flies

The writings of Skues had considerable influence on chalk stream angling in the first half of the twentieth century and this is reflected in Roger Woolley's fly lists. The two men corresponded over a period of time and Roger was specifically mentioned in *Nymph Fishing for Chalk Stream Trout* for his skills in entomology and fly-dressing. Woolley advises that, although tied for chalk stream trout these flies 'will kill on any river; are especially good on brooks if tied rather large.' These were lightly dressed flies required to sink on contact with the water. Rough Olive, Greenwell's Glory, Blue Dun, Iron Blue, Watery Dun, Hare's Ear and Black Gnat were the advertised patterns.

Nymphs for bulgers, underwater feeders, tailers

As nymph fishing advanced on the lines advocated by G E M Skues it became more popular with those who Woolley calls 'up-to-date flyfishermen'. Roger Woolley's interest in entomology gave him intimate knowledge of subsurface life forms which make up the greater proportion of the diets of both trout and grayling. He had long realised that, given appropriate weather and water conditions, anglers armed with imitations of these stood a good chance of sport throughout the season. He does make it very clear that this style of angling is no haphazard activity and has to be practiced in a skilled and thoughtful manner. The angler needs knowledge of the fish's feeding behaviour, the likely prey, an ability to cast accurately and judgement in calculating how fast the fly sinks. Management of the fishing depth needed to be accomplished by judicious greasing of the cast and the application of glycerine to the fly. Woolley thought that a nymph suitably presented to a feeding fish would seldom be refused, the indication of interest being a decided twitch to the cast – if only it were always that simple! The nymphs were dressed with either dubbed or quill bodies and he considered comparatively few patterns were required for a season's fishing.

Utility flies

'Utility' flies were advertised as being suitable to fish either wet or dry. They appear to have been another speciality of Woolley's which he felt met the requirements of the 'up-to-date' angler whose time on the water was limited and who wished to get the most out of time spent at the waterside. Flies were lightly dressed, standard imitations with longish, stiff, cock hackles giving transparency and lively play, when fished wet and increased floatation when fished dry. He suggests beginning the day's angling by choosing two seasonable utility patterns and fishing them wet over rough water, behind obstructions, close to banks and by tree roots on a short line, keeping in touch with the flies at all times. Should a rise occur the point fly is adjusted to match the naturals and oiled to fish dry. The dropper is left wet to 'fish itself'. When the rise ends the angler reverts to fishing both patterns wet until there is further surface activity.

A wide range of 'Utility' patterns were available including mayflies. The space and recommendations applied to these patterns is that of Roger Woolley the salesman giving the 'hard sell.'

Devonshire and West Country flies

Local fly-patterns brought Roger Woolley a considerable amount of work. Typical of these were the flies used on the steep, rough streams of the West Country. The patterns are similar in style to North Country Spiders but are dressed with stiff, bright cock hackles which work in the flow when fished across and down the stream. Woolley tied these flies with high quality undyed hackles whenever possible, those dressed with blue dun or brassy dun hackles being dearer on account of supply problems. His own particular recommended flies were Blue Upright, Red Spinner and Olive Upright. Three dozen standard patterns were advertised, among them dressings seldom heard of outside their locality – Pink Badger, Bastard's Fly, Prickman's Fly, Clumber Fancy and Edmond's Palmer. (Is this latter fly associated with Harfield H Edmonds, the North Country angler and author who, with Norman N Lee, wrote Brook and River Trouting in 1916?)

Yorkshire and North Country flies

The success of sparsely hackled North Country patterns was well-known to Roger Woolley. Almost certainly, as a fisher on the Dove, Manifold and Derwent, he would have had considerable experience of their use. Added to this were his visits to Yorkshire rivers where Spiders were, and still are, very widely used. He remarks that 'later on in the season the dry fly is, of late years, somewhat ousting them from favour.'

Roger was careful to tie these flies true to type, conscious they needed to be dressed sparsely with the minimum of soft hackle. However, he then proposes a departure of his own, beginning with the words 'It may be rank heresy on my part…' It almost certainly was heresy in the eyes of many North Country anglers for a Midlander to suggest dressing spiders with bright, stiff, sparkling cock hackles! He tied up a small stock of these specials in a dozen patterns and offered them on a trial basis with clients' orders. I have found no evidence of the results of this experiment.

All of the patterns described by Edmonds and Lee in *Brook and River Trouting* are offered in the catalogues along with other regularly fished patterns in similar style. The patterns of John Jackson, T E Pritt and Francis Walbran were available tied to order. He also lists a dressing of the Stone Fly Creeper. Traditionally, the large nymphs of the stonefly were collected and fished live in Derbyshire and Yorkshire but Woolley had seen the need and taken the opportunity to produce an imitation. Again, how successful this was is not recorded.

Welsh flies

A further series of lightly dressed flies for use on Welsh streams and rivers were produced tied to the specifications of local anglers. The flies are described as 'having a thin rakish look that at once sets them in a class of their own.' Woolley says that shop bought patterns had three times the amount of dressing there should be on a correctly made fly. Less well-known patterns listed include March Browns with yellow, brown green and gold bodies, Elan Red, Black Quill and Pupil Teacher.

Always quick to experiment and to take advantage of new developments Roger also tied a range of flies in the 'Glanrhos' style originated by Leonard Graham-Clarke, the wing and hackle of the fly being formed from the same hackle. This gave wet fly patterns 'delicacy and fineness of dressing'.

Dr. Hamilton's favourite flies for Irish waters

Despite Roger Woolley's time in Ireland his catalogues have a dearth of Irish fly patterns. It is possible there was not a large demand for them hence their absence. However a regular contributor to *Shooting Times* by the name of Dr. Hamilton gave Woolley a collection of his favoured patterns for inclusion in his lists, a cast of three described as a silver ribbed, blue bodied black hackle for tail fly, a silver grey for second and a small red hackle for top fly, and the Hare's Ear and Yellow, Black Ostrich, Ward's Infallible and a small Claret Fly. The collection is not included in the later catalogues.

Flies for Midland waters

Roger Woolley's selection of flies for his home waters had their roots in the dressings of Alfred Ronalds and David Foster. He mentions the works of both men – *The Fly-Fisher's Entomology* and *The Scientific Angler* – two volumes which were almost certainly in his bookcase. Both Ronalds and Foster were expert fishers of the Dove. He would have also probably known William and Wilfred, the son and grandson of David Foster and proprietors of tackle dealers 'Foster's of Ashbourne', as they were competitors of his in the business of serving anglers who fished on the upper and middle Dove.

Once more Woolley proposes some alteration to the dressing method to benefit his clients and perhaps to give his products greater appeal to anglers. He says that hackle-fibre winged flies were first trialled on Midland rivers, being a considerable improvement on ordinary wings and that he had every confidence in them for other waters too. Some four dozen patterns are listed including such local dressings as Cockwing Dun, Moss's Cockwing and Golden Earwig.

Flies for Scotland and the Borderland

A list of trout flies is offered which 'will give every satisfaction to anglers on Northern waters.' There are three dozen different patterns, most being standard dressings but with a number of less well-known dressings. Among these are Cairn's Fancy, Fenwick's Favourite, Grafton's Favourite, Laurie's Favourite, Johnston's Glory and Lee's Favourite.

E M Tod's patterns of wet flies

Woolley begins this section of his catalogue by quoting E M Tod's specification of wet fly structure. Patterns are very similar to those dressed in the Derbyshire-style – a thin body, sparse hackle and soft, thin upright wing. Woolley was very familiar with this style of fly, finding them effective in his own angling on the Derbyshire and Staffordshire waters. He tied up samples and sent them to Tod for inspection and comment – the reply received was complimentary, Tod assuring the fly-dresser that 'they were just the class of fly he would use himself.' Woolley's customers could order any pattern mentioned in Tod's book *Wet Fly Fishing* confident they had been approved and accurately tied to description.

Stewart's spiders

Once more, Woolley was very much on home-ground with these patterns. He had considerable expertise and understanding in the use and tying of this type of fly. He thought Spiders to be good imitations of various nymphs and stressed their success when fished upstream. He produced his own variations of W C Stewart's Spiders, extending the range of flies from the Black, Dun and Red Spiders of the originator. A further nine shades of nymphs were dressed by Woolley in the same way as the originals with the hackle turns running part way down the fly body. His additions to the range were Medium Olive, Dark Olive, March Brown, Greenwell, Iron Blue, Blue Dun, Blue Winged Olive, Pale Watery and Rough Olive all dressed as spiders.

Clyde flies

Little information is forthcoming from Woolley on the subject of these flies. He refers to them as 'peculiar dressings used chiefly on the Clyde, but are good on any clear, over-fished waters.' They are similar in style to the flies of Roger Woolley's native rivers being sparsely dressed and many having a thin upright wing. John Reid, writing in his book *Clyde Style Flies* (1971) describes them as having 'sombre hue and lack of gaudy embellishment.' There is no list of patterns given but those who regularly fished such local flies would be aware of the dressings they required. At the time Roger Woolley first advertised Clyde flies they were probably little known outside Scotland – their presence in the catalogues being an example of his entrepreneurial spirit.

Japanese flies

A further promotion was a range of flies based on dressings from Japan given to Roger by one of his 'patrons'. The source is not named but presumably was a person of some wealth or influence to be familiar with Japanese waters in the 1920s. Woolley does not seem too impressed by the quality of the flies, noting: 'The Japanese are a clever nation ... but I do not think they can teach us much about fly making or flyfishing.' He did however think they were worth a trial on British waters. The patterns he describes were wet flies tied up 'chiefly in brighter colours than our natural imitations of natural flies, and their chief feature is a blob of gold at head and tail which should prove attractive.' (A pity he did not go a little further with the development and call them 'Goldheads', he might have made a fortune!)

Grayling flies

A good deal of advice is dispensed about catching grayling on fly, all based on Roger Woolley's experience and observations. He was one of the greatest grayling anglers, valuing this species as a serious sporting challenge long before it became popular as such with most flyfishers. He spent years studying the fish – coming to the conclusion the 'Lady' was a fickle and fastidious opponent. When in pursuit of grayling Roger counselled anglers to take one day at a time, to lay down no plans, keep dry flies on the small side and to be aware that the fish can be very gut shy. He caught many more fish on fancy flies but favoured the use of natural imitations when a rise was in progress and found grayling would come for a small dry fly in the absence of naturals on the water.

In winter he used flies 'padded with lead' (some tied on double hooks), to search out the fish gathered in deep holes. 'A brace or two of grayling can be caught with fly on most days in winter.'

A list of three dozen patterns are offered, many of which were invented by Woolley. Bumbles and Witches feature, as do the Steel Blue and Roger's Fancy, two of his favourite patterns.

Sea-trout, loch and reservoir flies

A list of around one hundred flies is given under this title. Many are 'Series' patterns, Teal, Woodcock, Pheasant, Mallard, Jay, Bustard, Grouse and White Tip with the appropriate body colour following. The Pennell and General Eagles patterns are also included, as are the loch flies of R C Bridgett. Many of these flies are present in the fly book of Roger Woolley and the dressings are described in the relevant chapter. The reason given for the large number of patterns was that despite many of them being rarely used, all anglers have their own favourites. Woolley acknowledged the difficulties of fishing large, and in his day, comparatively thinly stocked waters saying that success largely depended on the skill of both angler and boatman but, using one of his promotional phrases, assures the reader that 'good flies get the best fish.' He again expresses the view that in difficult conditions bright hackles and sparsely dressed patterns have the edge over heavily dressed flies. Comment on reservoir fishing is limited to advising the use of smaller sizes of fly than on the lochs until later in the catalogues he discusses 'Blagdon Flies'.

Lt.-Col. Alban Wilson's Himalayan trout flies

Lt.-Colonel James Alban Wilson, D S O, wrote *Trout Fishing in Kashmir* which was published in 1920. Four years later he followed this with *Sport and Service in Assam and Elsewhere*. He served for 27 years in command of 1st battalion The Eighth Gurkhas. Tours of duty included Afghanistan, Mesopotamia and the North West Frontier regions. Lt Col Wilson was a client of Roger Woolley's, and he passed on to Roger the dressings of those patterns he found worked on the hill streams he fished throughout the sub-continent for both indigenous species, and the trout 'seeded' in the waters by colonists. Alban Wilson fished widely in India 'from Kashmir to Burma, as well as in the Central Provinces and the Nilgiris.' Soldiers and civil servants employed in India had both opportunity and resources to indulge in many sporting activities and supplying their angling requisites was probably a worthwhile part of Woolley's business. He provided exact copies of Wilson's patterns which were Large Brown, My Fancy, Kashmir Summer Dun, Shimong Yellow, Abor Dun, Kashmir Dun, Dark Red and White Ant. The latter, recommended fished dry, is as good a fly as is the 'Green Drake in the British Isles.' The dressings, unfortunately not detailed, may have been more complex than other patterns or may simply have had a 'colonial premium' applied to them. Whatever, they cost considerably more than many other selections.

Alban Wilson's UK home was at West Burton in the Yorkshire Dales – rivers such as the Cover, Ure and Wharfe would have provided a change from those of India.

Mr Percy Lloyd's One Fly for all the Season

At two shillings a dozen in 1920 this was one of Roger's more expensive dressings. Percy Lloyd was an angler of great experience on Welsh brooks and wrote to the *Fishing Gazette* describing the success of his fly. It had been the subject of wagers and had always delivered victory for its originator. It was styled 'Lloyd's Beauty' by many of its adherents.

Hook :	No. 2 sneck bronze
Body :	'Lightish'
Hackle :	'Small blue'

H Garnet Rolf, who used the fly, said that it also had a peculiarly coloured orange tag and the the body and hackle are somewhat the colour of the Little Marryat. This too was published in the *Fishing Gazette* and included in some of his catalogues by Roger Woolley.

Personal dressings of other anglers are also included in some lists. Roger was given a sample of 'The famous Pheasant Tail Fly' by its originator Mr Payne-Collier to copy and distribute. The pattern was invented around the turn of the 19th and 20th centuries and had a considerable reputation. Woolley also supplied a variant with a lighter, brassier, shade of hackle. He noted 'both kill well.'

Roger was also able to obtain patterns of Mr G Garrow-Green's Black Hackle Nos. 1 and 2. These flies Woolley describes as peculiarly tied flies and are recommended in the catalogue as successful, both wet and dry.

Garrow-Green was the author of *Trout Fishing in Brooks, Its Science and Art,* published in 1920.

'Kingsmo' special pattern of flies for lake brown trout and sea-trout

Roger Woolley describes these patterns as being designed for use as dropper flies when lake fishing. Their development was the result of many years' work and experiment by 'an amateur fly-dresser'. Their originator is not named, but is almost certainly T C Kingsmill Moore, the author of *A Man May Fish*, who created a set of Irish 'Bumbles' for use on lakes and loughs for brown and sea-trout fishing. They were intended to suggest surface fly activity such as the movement created by sedges, crane flies and similar terrestrials – 'no attempt is made to imitate any particular specimen of surface life, but the characteristics of surface life itself.' In the course of his experiments T C Kingsmill Moore found that Derbyshire bumbles had something of the transparency he sought and formed the opinion that they were the most effective style of dropper fly, though long neglected.

The flies he created accentuated the transparency and glitter caused by movement on the surface, in a subtle way helped by the use of different coloured hackles wound together and the use of tinsel or seal's fur bodies. His results were flies which combined the quiet translucence of Irish flies with the Palmer or Bumble style and found to be very effective.

The patterns offered by Roger Woolley are briefly described and similar in name and dressing to those of Kingsmill Moore. Roger Woolley always sought the permission and approval of those whose patterns he sold, usually naming them. Perhaps it was not professional for the name of a High Court judge to be used in a fishing catalogue, hence 'Kingsmo'.

Dace and chub flies

Flyfishing for coarse fish, especially dace and chub, was a popular form of sport and within the financial reach of many unable to afford access to trout streams. Good watercraft, stealth and fast reactions were required to catch these species consistently, the favoured time being on hot summer days. Roger advertised his 'special' Dace Fly as being 'the most deadly fly on the market for these fish.' It was fished dry, the main requirement being accuracy in casting to present the fly without alarming the quarry.

The pattern was offered in two colours, red and black.

Body :	Peacock herl, ribbed flat gold
Tag :	White wool or feather
Hackle :	Red cock, or, for a change, black cock
Hook :	00 to 0

Further suggestions for dace include Wickham's Fancy, Red Tag, Little Chap, The Witch, Black Gnat, Red Spinner, small Coachman and various midges.

The dace flies tied in larger sizes, Bumbles, Palmers, Alexandra, Coch-y-Bondhu and Coachman were Roger Woolley's favoured patterns for chub fishing. He advocated the addition of a white tag of wool or kid to those patterns which did not already sport one.

Night flies

Night fishing for trout was an approved means of catching larger cannibal trout in the north and west of the country and also in Wales, but not so on chalk streams or limestone rivers. Large moths and Bustards in red, brown white and yellow were the chosen lures of many but Woolley extended his range to include the Governor, Wickham's and Coachman. A fourth pattern, the Sweep, I had not come across before. Leonard West lists the dressing in *The Natural Trout Fly and its Imitation* (1912). He says it is often mistakenly called the Hawthorn Fly. The dressing is given here:

Hook :	0 – 2
Horns :	Black cock
Legs :	Black cock
Thorax :	Black ostrich
Body :	Short black ostrich
Rib :	Silver wire
Notes :	An odd turn of iridescent hackle at the shoulder.

Woolley supplied an approved range of Leonard West's fly-dressings. Many of these were marked 'g' in some catalogues as being good flies for grayling, a subject very close to the dresser's heart.

The Sweep is also listed by Tom Stewart in *Two Hundred Popular Flies* (1979) as a salmon or sea-trout fly:

Tail :	Small golden pheasant topping or tippet
Body :	Black floss silk, ribbed with oval gold tinsel
Hackle :	Black 'henny' cock tied as beard
Wing :	From any hard-wearing black wing feather, crow or cock
Cheeks :	Blue kingfisher or bright blue hackle tips

Blagdon flies and lures

Blagdon reservoir in Somerset opened for angling around 1900 and provided some of the first stocked reservoir fishing in the country. It proved to be fertile water, gaining a considerable reputation for the size and quality of its fish. Roger Woolley describes it thus: 'Fishing for the big trout at Blagdon reservoir is quite a sport on its own, and special patterns of flies have been invented to tempt the big brown and rainbow trout.' He proposed the use of small salmon flies such as Doctors, Thunder and Lightning, Dusty Miller and Silver Grey to imitate the large numbers of sticklebacks available to the trout, other useful flies being Claret and Mallard, Invicta, Raider and Alexandra.

Evidently night fishing was enjoyed at Blagdon, the accepted technique being the use of big tandem flies with two or three hooks. Compared with other flies in his lists these were quite expensive. In

Woolley's notes he says the largest trout were caught on these, one of his clients catching 26 trout weighing a total of 156 pounds in one season.

Other methods were successful at Blagdon. There were vast numbers of midge larvae present in the water and regular anglers like Willie Cox experimented with new fly-dressings. From these experiments flies such as the Blagdon Green Midge and the Blagdon Buzzer were developed. It is surprising that Roger Woolley chose to supply dressings of the large lures and not imitations of natural flies.

Salmon flies

Roger dressed salmon flies to client's specifications or from lists of standard dressings. In his fly book there are a number of small salmon patterns and one large salmon iron the name of which my research has been unable to uncover.

He offered another service appertaining to salmon flies of the time. Many anglers still fished with gut-eyed flies which became worn in use and these could be renovated. He also re-tied those with broken hooks and dressing damage. The saving to the angler was considerable and Woolley asked that such flies be sent during the winter months when pressure of work was lower. The flies were taken to pieces, feathers saved and retied on the 'new' fly. Replacement of expensive feathers resulted in the repair costing a few pence more. It is interesting that even in the 1920s jungle cock and golden pheasant toppings were specified as 'expensive'.

'Dear Sir,

I thank you for the re-tied salmon flies to hand this morning. They are admirably repaired, and the price is most reasonable. I am sending you 50 more by this post. Please re-tie these at your convenience on the same excellent up-eyed hooks that you used for the others.

Yours Truly,
F. M. D.'

Casts of various qualities were stocked and a further service was provided in the shape of mounted trout and grayling casts, consisting of casts with two or three flies attached. Brook, river or lake patterns were available with appropriate variations for the height of the water and brightness of the day. Casts were suited to the water fished by the client, Woolley being in touch with expert anglers throughout Britain and Ireland.

Further information about new products was provided by Roger Woolley in the form of loose-leaf insert sheets.

Up-to-date flies

Roger Woolley's insert sheets in his catalogues indicate a very real change in conditions on the rivers from his youth. He comments on this fact in 'Up-to-date flies', saying the big fly hatches of the past had disappeared. Further, he noted that fishing the dry fly often results in no fish at all. Reasons he gives for changes in the sport include greatly increased angling pressure, but perhaps even more significant, rain washings from tarred roads, a topic he comments upon several times in his writings. Presumably, limestone road surfaces of the past allowed less run off as they were porous, or such run-off as occurred was neutral or even beneficial to flora and fauna of rivers. Whatever the case, Roger Woolley seems certain that fly life in the rivers was fundamentally damaged. Leonard West, writing in *The Natural Trout Fly and its Imitation* at a similar time mentions pollution in respect of mayfly hatches. He suggests a failure of mayfly to appear in good numbers may be the result of this as their development as nymphs takes three years; one incident of pollution would therefore affect several batches of nymphs.

Woolley's answer to the angling problems these conditions produced was to use differently dressed flies and an intelligent combination of dry, wet and sunk fly methods of fishing. These, combined with the individual angler's local knowledge of quarry and water and a skilful approach, would result in success. In addition, fly-dressers and anglers had contrived patterns which were not specific imitators. These flies, by means of form, colour and movement, attracted both trout and grayling.

Woolley advised that the angler should begin to fish with two wet flies in the absence of rising fish and using these, appropriate places are searched for quarry. Should fish begin to show, substitution of the point fly with a suitable imitation is required. Should both methods fail, then resort is made to leaded patterns which may yield fish from the depths. It is also worthwhile to try the dry fly if that is the angler's preference. The patterns advised are high-riding with long hackle, such as Woolley's camouflaged patterns and variants. According to water conditions and weather, these were often found worthwhile despite there not being a rise.

Roger Woolley's 'Up-to-date' patterns are listed as:

Purely wet flies – slightly leaded

March Brown Spider, Greenwell Spider, Rough Olive Spider, Carrot Fly, Olive Nymph, and Fry Fly. ('The Fry Fly has a gold or a silver body, very lightly hackled with stiff clear cock to give a transparent effect or with a very soft, downy hackle for movement, and effectively imitates the tiny fry of the minnow.')

J C Mottram, writing in *Fly Fishing Some New Arts and Mysteries* (1915) details a pattern also called the Fry Fly, which was very useful at Blagdon reservoir. The pattern advertised by Roger Woolley may be a modification of Mottram's fly, which used turkey and gull down for its body. Later in his catalogues, Roger Woolley advertises flies suitable for this water.

Rough water flies – wet or dry

Special Pheasant Tail, Steel Blue, Paddy's Fancy Nos. 1 and 2, Half Stone Variant, Lake's Fly, and Red Beetle. These flies can be used wet or dry, and are to be fished 'in or on the streams.' The Steel Blue was Woolley's favourite pattern and Lake's Fly, the invention of Richard Lake, Woolley's co-author (of *The Grayling*). The Red Eyed Derby Beetle, also known as The Derbyshire Belle is a popular pattern on the county's rivers. It sports a red tail, peacock herl body, black hackle and red bead eyes.

Bright day flies – wet or dry

Golden Pheasant Tail, Brown Doctor, Orange Curlew and Red and Gold – these were tied on smaller hooks for use in low clear water and bright weather conditions.

Camouflaged dry flies

March Brown, Hare's Ear, Olive Hare's Ear, Blue Dun, Olive Dun, Red Spinner – little information is given as to how they differ from standard patterns. There is a suggestion that they may have had longer hackles than normal.

This insert concludes:
'Help in every way you can all movements against pollution of our rivers, or soon there will be no fishing at all for us, or for those that follow us.'

Lightly dressed dry flies

These patterns Roger Woolley advertised as 'The Flies for the Expert'. He thought the increased popularity of dry fly angling resulted in fish becoming cautious, the constant casting conspiring to make trout very wary. Heavily hackled patterns were considered necessary by most anglers in order to allow the fly to float for more than a short time. What was gained in buoyancy was lost in realism in regard to the natural insects. Woolley's lightly dressed flies sought to remedy this problem for those who wished to fish a dainty fly. He claimed such flies had not been offered previously and recommended them on the strengths of their close imitation to naturals and sparse dressings. They were winged in such a manner as to ensure they 'cocked' on the water, fine wire hooks cut down weight but, as a result of this, care was advised when playing fish. Woolley stressed the fly only needed to float on the surface for three or four feet in order to cover a fish and these patterns were well capable of remaining afloat to achieve this given an accurate cast and good presentation. When fishing rough water it was necessary to grease cast as well as line.

Duns were offered either winged or hackled, spinners hackled only. The latter could be purchased with two styles of body, rough or smooth and shiny. The smooth body seems to have been favoured by Woolley, the seal's fur version 'much liked by some experts as giving greater translucency than any other material'.

A summary of a season's angling with these patterns:

March – April: March Brown; Early Olive Duns
April – May: Iron Duns for cold days and again in
                         October for grayling
April onwards for the season: Olive Duns
May onwards for the season: Blue Winged Olives; Pale Watery
                         Duns, particularly in the evening
May – June: Alder fly
Through summer: Black Gnat; Long Legged Gnat

A further innovation was lightly-dressed wet flies in the 'Utility' range. These were dressed on midge sized double hooks and 'They will please you and certainly bring you some fish in low clear water.' These flies were tied with high quality cock hackles.

Roger Woolley's publications

Roger Woolley wrote two books and contributed to a third (*The Grayling* with Richard Lake). The former two resulted from articles first appearing in the *Fishing Gazette*. The first was *Modern Trout Fly Dressing*, the second, *The Fly-Fisher's Flies*. By the time the articles were written Roger Woolley's reputation was firmly established nationally as a fly-dresser and grayling fisherman. Whether he was invited to produce the articles by R B Marston, then editor of the *Fishing Gazette*, or whether he offered them as a speculative exercise is not clear. Whatever the circumstances, they were enthusiastically received by the readers.

Both volumes are written in a clear readable style. All instruction relating to fly-dressing is presented in a sequential order which is easy to follow and implement. A nightmare for many anglers, the morass of entomology, is simplified into a concise and understandable system set down in the terms of the layman.

Modern Trout Fly Dressing

This book was published in the *Fishing Gazette Angler's Library* series in 1932. It is based on the articles Roger Woolley wrote for the *Fishing Gazette* in 1931 as *A Treatise on Fly Tying*. It was advertised in January 1933 at six shillings, by post 6s 4d – from Roger Woolley, Hatton, Derby or Book Department, The Fishing Gazette, 56-58, Whitcomb Street, London, W.C.2.

Modern Trout Fly Dressing was an important primary source of new fly patterns running to three editions in 1932, 1939 and 1950. Over four hundred dressings are detailed, a large number of them being invented and developed by Roger Woolley. He had considerable influence on fly-dressing during his lifetime both in terms of methods and new patterns. G E M Skues and Arthur Ransome advised anglers to refer to Woolley's writings in their respective publications, *Nymph Fishing for Chalk Stream Trout* (1939) and *Mainly about Fishing* (1959). A more recent recommendation comes from

A typical First Edition of *Modern Trout Fly Dressing*

Sylvester Nemes in *Two Centuries of Soft-Hackled Flies* published in 2004. Nemes wrote that, excepting the works of T E Pritt and Edmonds and Lee, no other work 'offers so much knowledge about, and instruction on, tying soft hackled flies.'

Modern Trout Fly Dressing is a concise flyfisherman's handbook which outlines the life histories of aquatic and terrestrial insects of interest to the angler in simple and sequential terms. The techniques of fly-dressing are broken down into sections beginning with materials, tools and dyes. Tying of bodies, different styles of wings and legs is dealt with in

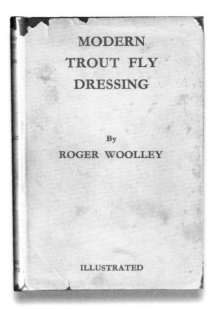

A copy of *Modern Trout Fly Dressing* complete with its seldom-seen dust-jacket

much detail, followed by more specific instructions regarding the construction of wet and dry flies. This includes groups such as nymphs, spiders, bumbles and mayflies.

Fly-dressings of natural insects, duns and spinners, sedges, stoneflies, mayflies and various terrestrials are listed and where applicable, regional variations offered. Some of these dressings are those developed by Roger Woolley, his clients or associates.

General and fancy dry flies, variants and wet fly dressings, traditional dressings from the North and West are also listed. Some of these are dressings whose originators allowed him to dress and publish their patterns in his catalogues and books. There are chapters of grayling flies, loch and sea-trout patterns, the text being rounded up with chub and dace dressings and finally a comprehensive index.

Life-size black and white sketches of the representative insect groups are included on a fold out sheet. In addition there are many figures in black and white which give the impression of having been based on photographs. These are used to illustrate the fly-dressing techniques. A hook gauge is included as the frontispiece illustration in which the hooks are shown life size. Some of the illustrations are rather dark and lacking in sharpness, a point made by G E M Skues in his otherwise complimentary remarks about Roger Woolley's work, but nevertheless are better than none.

The Fly-Fisher's Flies

Again the result of a series of articles in the *Fishing Gazette – The Fly-Fisher's Flies* was also published in three editions: 1938, 1948 and 1950. This book expands on the brief introduction and descriptions of natural flies in his first book, *Modern Trout Fly Dressing*. Each group of insects, or specific flies, are described in more detail, appearance, habitat and life history all being carefully discussed in simple language. Once more Roger Woolley's observational skill is apparent – the behaviour of nymphs, duns and spinners all being described, often with the reaction of the fish to their presence on the water. Size, shape and colour are the criteria Woolley uses to determine each species or group.

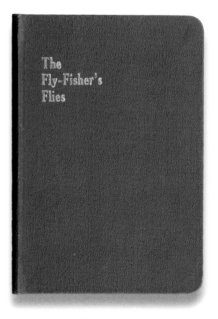

The Fly-Fisher's Flies

Life-size black and white line drawings serve to illustrate the text, and whilst they are rather primitive stylistically, they highlight the main features of each insect very adequately. The shape, veining, translucence and patterns of wings are shown – where necessary shading is used to suggest blocks of darker colour on the bodies.

The book is a specific identification manual for use at the waterside by anglers who are not of an entomological bent. It is presented in the simplest way whilst retaining vital information to identify more than thirty different insects and their several life stages. However it does require the angler to go out and to use it, applying the content to his or her own waters. It is unlikely that all the creatures described are going to be present on any one particular water, and certainly not at the same time. Consequently the process of familiarising oneself with each species is simplified further.

An appendix entitled '*Artificial Flies to Use when the Natural Fly is on*' is a useful addition to the book and there is a comprehensive index.

Here is a summary of the appendix taken from *The Fly-Fisher's Flies*:

Natural Fly	Artificials
Spring Olive Dun :	Spring Olive Dun; Rough Olive; Blue Dun; Dark Blue Upright; Waterhen Bloa; Spring Hare's Ear; Dark Greenwell's Glory.
March Brown :	Any local March Brown pattern; Woodcock and Hare's Ear.
Iron-Blue Dun :	Iron-Blue Dun; Iron-Blue Quill; Dark Watchet; Snipe and Purple; Infallible.
Dark Olive Dun :	Dark Olive Dun; Dark Olive Quill; Greenwell's Glory; Small Waterhen Bloa; Snipe and Yellow.
Medium Olive Dun :	Medium Olive Dun; Medium Olive Quill; Gold-Ribbed Hare's Ear; Summer Greenwell's Glory; Olive Bloa; Olive Upright.
Alder Fly :	'A hackled pattern tied with a good brownish-dun game cock hackle.'
Mayfly :	Wood Duck; the Major; the Lawrence; the Colonel; the Black Drake; the Spent Drake.
Blue-Winged Olive Dun :	Blue-Winged Olive Dun; Blue-Winged Olive Quill; Poult Bloa; hackled Blue-Winged Olive.
Pale Watery Dun :	Pale Watery Quill; Little Marryat; Ginger Quill; Autumn Dun; Small Blue Upright.

More Duns:	Turkey Brown; Claret Dun; Yellow May Dun; July Dun; August Dun.
Sedges :	Welshman's Button; Grannom; Silverhorns; Light, Medium and Dark Sedges; Silver Sedge; Orange Sedge.
Stone Fly :	Winged or hackled Stone Fly.
February Red :	Winged or hackled February Red
Early Brown :	Early Brown; Winter Brown; Dark Woodcock and Orange.
Yellow Sally :	Winged or hackled Yellow Sally.
Willow Fly :	Willow Fly; Brown Owl; Light Woodcock and Orange; Orange Partridge.
Needle Fly :	Needle Fly; Dark Needle; Spanish Needle.

The Grayling

The Grayling was published in 1942, with a revised edition in 1943, reprinted in 1946. Its author was a surgeon, Richard Lake, who described various aspects of the species. Its natural history is outlined followed by brief remarks on whether or not grayling should be introduced into trout streams. Fishing for grayling, their behaviour when hooked and the rise of the fish follow. He discusses the fish in relation to what they may see of their food and the angler pursuing them. An analysis of mouth structure and how this affects hooking followed by their food preferences and a number of autopsy results from fish caught in various rivers.

For the second edition (1943) Lake invited Woolley to contribute two practical chapters on fly and bait fishing for grayling. The first deals with dry and wet fly, the second with bait fishing. Woolley makes it clear he much prefers the fly over bait but nevertheless thoroughly details the latter method. He again uses some material from his previous writings from the *Fishing Gazette* though the notes on bait fishing are new.

It would seem the two men had been acquainted over a considerable period of time before publication of *The Grayling*. Roger Woolley's early catalogues include a pattern called 'Lake's Fly'. It is quite possible that Richard Lake was a long time client of Woolley.

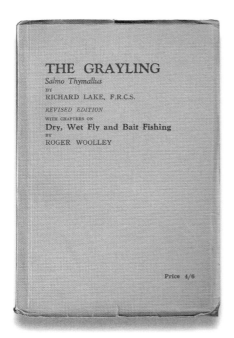

THE GRAYLING

Salmo Thymallus

BY

RICHARD LAKE, F.R.C.S.

REVISED EDITION

WITH CHAPTERS ON

Dry, Wet Fly and Bait Fishing

BY

ROGER WOOLLEY

Price 4/6

The Grayling, Revised Edition

Describing flies he used for grayling, Richard Lake writes 'My own list would include Blue Winged Olive, Ginger Quill, Tupp, my own fly (dressed by Roger Woolley), Iron Blue, Infallible Nymph, (weighted)'.

Unfortunately neither man records the dressing, it simply being listed under 'Up-to-date flies' for rough water, wet or dry.

The 'Grasshopper' bait receives some attention from Lake. The device is described, as is the means of fishing it, but Lake never used it. There are diagrams of the Grasshopper as made up by Roger Woolley, and they are quite remarkable objects with flying treble hooks, glass beads and bright silk covered lead bodies. Not content with all this, the odd maggot or two was often put on the hook by the angler. The inclusion of this lure may have been for the purpose of completion as it is unlikely either Richard Lake or Roger Woolley would have enjoyed catching grayling on such an object. Brief mention is given to spinning and minnow fishing, Lake recording that he once caught a grayling from the Teviot on a fly-spoon. *The Grayling* concludes with recipes from Charles Cotton and Richard Lake.

BIBLIOGRAPHY

Dates given are for first editions only. Dates of further editions, further bibliographical details, and second-hand copies can be obtained from Coch-y-Bonddu Books.

Garrow Green, G   *Trout Fishing in Brooks, Its Science and Art.*
                         Routledge, 1920
Hewitt, E R   *Telling on the Trout.* Scribner's, 1926
Hill, Raymond   *Wings and Hackle.* Horwood, 1912
Hills, J W   *A History of Fly Fishing for Trout.* Allan, 1921
Hutchinson, Horace G   *Fishing.* Country Life Library of Sport, 1904
Kingsmill-Moore, T C   *A Man May Fish.* Herbert Jenkins, 1960
Knowles, Christopher   *Orange Otter.* Medlar Press, 2006
Lake, Richard   *The Grayling.* Wilding & Son, 1942
Mackenzie, Gregor   *Memoirs of a Ghillie.* David and Charles, 1978.
Mee, Arthur   *Staffordshire*
Mosley, Sir Oswald   *History of the Castle, Priory and Town of Tutbury.*
                         London 1832

Mosley, Sir Oswald &
Brown, Edwin   *The Natural History of Tutbury.* London, 1863
Nemes, Sylvester   *Two Centuries of Soft Hackled Flies.*
                         Stackpole Books, 2004
Platts, W Carter   *Modern Trout Fishing.* A & C Black, 1938
Platts, W Carter   *Grayling Fishing.* A & C Black, 1939
Overfield, Donald T   *Famous Flies and their Originators.*
                         A & C Black, 1972
Overfield, Donald T   *50 Favourite Dry Flies.* Ernest Benn, 1980
Overfield, Donald T   *50 Favourite Wet Flies.* Ernest Benn, 1986
Ransome, Arthur   *Mainly About Fishing.* A & C Black 1959
Skues, G E M   *Nymph Fishing for Chalk Stream Trout.*
                         A & C Black, 1939
Stewart, Tom   *Two Hundred Popular flies.* Ernest Benn 1979

Taverner, Eric	*Trout Fishing from all Angles.*
	Lonsdale Library, 1950
Tod, E M	*Wet Fly Fishing.* Sampson, Low and Marston, 1903
Veniard, E	*500 Fly Dressings.* E Veniard, 1985
Veniard, John	*Reservoir and Lake Flies.* A & C Black, 1978
Walker, C F	*Fly Tying as an Art.* Herbert Jenkins, 1957
Watson, J N	*Angling with the Fly.*
	Ken Smith Publishing, 2008
West, Leonard	*The Natural Trout Fly and its Imitation.*
	Wm Potter, Liverpool 1921
Woolley, Roger	*Modern Trout Fly Dressing.* Fishing Gazette, 1932
Woolley, Roger	*The Fly-Fisher's Flies.* Fishing Gazette, 1938

Catalogues

Woolley, Roger. *A List of Special Trout and Grayling Flies.*
Parker, Printer, Burton; circa 1921; 1925; 1934; 1936.
Also that of Rosa Smith under the same title, circa 1960's.

Journals

Angling.	T K Wilson, 'The Story Behind the Fancy,'
Fly Fishing and Fly Tying	August 2006 Published information request
Unknown magazine cutting.	Article by Hilda Brown, 'Give me a Witch and a Steel Blue,' Date unknown, circa late 1950's.
Trout & Salmon magazine.	Article by Donald T Overfield, Vol. 17; No. 198; December 1971
Trout & Salmon magazine.	August 2006 Published information request

Other Sources

Bailey, Aubrey.	*The Story of Artificial Fly Dressing and Trout Fishing* Unpublished 1975
Bailey, Aubrey	*Tutbury, Parts 1, 2 and 3.* Privately published
Wilson, T K	*Oakden's Claret,* Unpublished manuscript

APPENDICES

Help in every way you can all movements against pollution of our rivers or soon there will be no fishing at all for us, or those that follow us — Roger Woolley Catalogue

Appendix 1

Roger Woolley's favourite fly patterns

1. **Steel Blue**
    Hook :   Sizes 1 – 2
    Body :   Thin peacock herl, ribbed gold wire, with three turns of orange silk at tail end
    Hackle : Well grizzled bright blue cock, from shoulder to tail

2. **Grayling Witch**
    Hook :   Sizes 000 – 1
    Body :   Green peacock herl, ribbed flat silver
    Tag :   Red floss
    Hackle : Pale or medium blue dun
    (This fly is generally attributed to Roger Woolley and is almost certainly his own development and variant of the Witch series.)

Fancy grayling patterns recommended by Roger Woolley

3. **Bradshaw's Fancy**
    Hook :   Sizes 00 – 1
    Body :   Bronze peacock herl, with tag of red floss at head and tail
    Hackle : Norwegian crow

4.   **White Witch**
   Hook :   Sizes 00 – 3
   Body :   Green peacock herl, silver tipped and ribbed silver wire
   Tag :   Red floss
   Hackle :   White cock from shoulder to tail

5.   **Red Badger**
   Hook :   Sizes 00 – 1
   Body :   Red floss, ribbed silver wire and silver tipped
   Hackle :   Badger cock, from shoulder to tail

6.   **Silver Badger**
   Hook :   Sizes 0 – 1
   Body :   Silver tinsel with red tag at head and tail
   Hackle :   Badger hen

7.   **Red Tag**
   Hook :   Sizes 00 – 1
   Body :   Bronze peacock herl, with tip of gold or silver under tag
   Tag :   Red floss
   Hackle :   Red hen

8.   **Roger's Fancy**
   Hook :   Sizes 00 – 2
   Body :   Pale blue heron herl, ribbed fine flat silver, with red floss tag at
                 head and tail
   Hackle :   Pale blue hen

According to T K Wilson, writing in *Angling* magazine this pattern is a variant, devised in 1908 by Roger Woolley 'to provide a change from the Grayling Witch.' Woolley tried it out with success on both the Dove and the Test. He used it both dry and wet, the former tied small and fished early in the grayling season. As a wet fly it is best used from October to December. Some examples of the pattern have the tags wrapped on the hook.

9.   **Tommy's Favourite**

Hook :   Sizes 00 – 1

Body :   Quill from a yellow-blue macaw tail feather, the yellow to show as body the blue flue as a rib

Tag :   Red floss, tip of silver tinsel under tag

Hackle :   Medium blue hen

Patterns recommended by Roger Woolley for trout and grayling.

10.   **Burton Blue**

Hook :   Sizes 0 – 1

Body :   Waxed yellow tying silk, ribbed fine flat gold

Hackle :   Medium blue hen

Wings :   Formed from the feather from a water hen's breast

11.   **Burton Gold Spinner**

Hook :   Sizes 0 – 1

Body :   Waxed yellow tying silk, ribbed fine flat gold

Hackle :   Ginger hen

Wings :   Starling

12.   **Rough Olive**

Hook :   Sizes 1 – 2

Body :   Heron's herl dyed olive, ribbed gold wire

Hackle & Whisks :   Dark olive cock

Wings :   Dark starling or hen blackbird

13.   **Blue Badger**

(As Red Badger but with blue floss body.)

14.   **Silver Twist**

Hook :   Sizes 0 – 2

Body :   Blue fur, ribbed silver twist

Hackle :   Medium blue dun hen from shoulder to tail

15. **Brunton's Fancy**
    Hook :   Sizes 00 – 1
    Body :   Three turns gold twist at tail end, remainder green peacock herl
    Tag :   Indian crow feather
    Hackle :   Badger cock

16. **Rough Bumble**
    Hook :   Sizes 0 – 2
    Body :   Yellow floss, ribbed peacock herl and red silk
    Hackle :   Medium blue dun hen from shoulder to tail

17. **Mulberry Bumble**
    Hook :   Sizes 0 – 2
    Body :   Mulberry coloured floss, ribbed peacock herl
    Hackle :   Honey dun hen from shoulder to tail

18. **Light Bumble**
    Hook :   Sizes 0 – 2
    Body :   Pale yellow floss, ribbed peacock herl and red silk
    Hackle :   Pale dun hen from shoulder to tail

19. **Grey Palmer**
    Hook :   Sizes 0 – 2
    Body :   Black floss, ribbed silver wire
    Hackle :   Badger cock from shoulder to tail

Imitation Duns

Blue Dun
Iron Blue Dun   *standby of fly fishermen*
Blue Winged Olive
Pale Watery
July Dun
August Dun
Early Spring Olive

General Dry Flies

Pheasant Tail Spinner   *Suitable for any brown-red spinner*
Rusty Spinner   *Imitates Blue Winged Olive Spinner*

Flies which imitate Pale Olive and Pale Watery Duns

Pale Evening Dun
Whitchurch Dun (Halford)
Driffield Dun
Ginger Quill
Yellow Quill
Cinnamon Quill
Yellow Dun
Ash Dun
Autumn Dun
Little Pale Blue Dun
Flight's Fancy
Golden Dun
(This last pattern was a fly which David Foster of Ashbourne claimed to have invented. There was much dispute about this, including remarks by W H Foster in The Scientific Angler.*)*

Pike Scale Black Gnat   *First catch your pike…*
Hofland's Fancy   *Red spinners*

When late rises to unknown spinners occur choose the spinner of the hatch of the day.

Sedges

Woolley thought that sedges were under-used by anglers but considered a few patterns covered most needs.

Welshman's Button
Grannom
Silver-horns   *Black, brown and olive*

Stoneflies

February Red   *Early season*
Winter Brown
Willow Fly   *August and September*
Needle Fly

Various

Alder   *Fish wet, useful when fish not taking available Mayflies*
March Brown   *Universal Fly'. Use whether natural present or not*
Cow Dung   *Worth a try on windy days when stock are present*
Hawthorn   *Excellent when in season*
Oak Fly   *Good on brooks*
Black Gnats
Midges   *Good when few naturals are on the water*
Ants   *Invaluable when they occur, always carry some*
Beetles
Long Legged Gnats   *Always on the water, in absence of duns worth a trial*

Appendix 2

Colloquial names of fly-dressing materials used by Roger Woolley

Mallard Blues	*Purple Mallard*
White Tipped Blues	*White Tip*
Red Ibis	*Ibis*
Hooded Crow	*Norwegian Crow*
Hare Flax	*Long stout hairs from down a hare's back*

Appendix 3

List of cartoons by L P Morinan used in Woolley's catalogues, dated and signed as below.

1933   Steeplejack on Church. L Morinan.
          Obtaining Roger Wooley (*sic*) Hackles. L P Morinan.
          Piscator and Fishmonger. L P Morinan.
          Bridge Trout. L P M.
          Club Meeting. L P M.
          Major and Newcomer. L M.

1932   Roger Wooley (*sic*) Fly Factory 1. L M.
          Monk and Pedlar. L M.
          Loch Ness Monster. L M.
          Judge Summing Up. L M.

1936   Boy Caught Fishing. L M.

Undated   Motorist and Shepherd. L M.
            Worms and Minnows. L M.

Undated and Unsigned Three Anglers and their Catch.

Appendix 4

Fly-dressing materials favoured by Roger Woolley

Hackles
    Blue Andalusian
    Brassy Dun   *Smoky-blue centre, brassy tips*
    Honey Dun
    Rusty Dun   *Blue dun well flecked with rust coloured speckles*
Heron herl
Horsehair
Raffia
Seal's fur
Wheat straw

Appendix 5

Another collection of patterns

The following flies are part of a collection associated with Roger Woolley. It is impossible to say whether or not the patterns were tied by Roger Woolley or by his dressers but the collection is certainly of sufficient importance to warrant inclusion in this book. There are two designations of folder which may relate to their age:

Trout and Grayling Flies
From
Roger Woolley
Angler & Fly-dresser
Tutbury
Burton-on-Trent

The other being -

Best flies kill most fish
Get your
Trout and Grayling Flies
From
Roger Woolley & Co
Anglers and Fly-dressers
Tutbury
Burton-on-Trent

227

The latter folder is printed *Roger Woolley & Co., Anglers and Fly-dressers*. This was the company style used after Roger took his daughters into partnership in an official capacity. *Roger Woolley, Angler and Fly-dresser* suggests him working on his own at an earlier stage of the business. The printing on some fly folders is in red rather than black ink, though this does not appear to have any significance regarding date.

It is perhaps worthy of note that other folders, not in this collection, have the 'Marston Road, Hatton, Derby', address which perhaps indicate their being later still. It may well be, of course, that in the interests of economy, fly folders were used irrespective of the niceties of their title; Roger Woolley was not a man to waste anything! The named patterns contained in the former folders have been included in the appropriate chapter with their titles and dressings. The remainder of the collection is probably flies tied by, or under the auspices of, Woolley – though there is no absolute provenance for this. They are in the style of Woolley and among them are patterns associated with him: witches, bumbles, midge doubles and small alders. There are also several hackled mayflies, Roger's favoured style of dressing and fishing the fly.

Hackled Flies

1.   *Hook* :   0 to gut
        Whisks : Speckled partridge
        Body :   Light olive or yellow floss silk ribbed 4 turns claret silk
        Hackle : Brown speckled partridge

2.   *Hook* :   0 to gut, sneck
        Body :   Grey-brown dubbing, possibly rabbit fur,
                  ribbed 4 turns yellow silk
        Hackle : Long dun hen

3.   *Hook* :   2 sneck, down-eyed
        Body :   Flat gold tinsel
        Hackle : Speckled brown partridge

Bumbles and Witches

1.   Mulberry Bumble Variant
    Hook :   1 – 2 sneck, down-eyed
    Body :   Mulberry silk ribbed 4 turns peacock herl
    Hackle :   Long, at shoulder only, Dark blue dun cock

2.   Grey Palmer
    Hook :   0 down-eyed
    Body :   Black silk
    Hackle :   Palmered badger cock, ribbed silver wire

3.   Red Palmer
    Hook :   2 to gut
    Body :   Red wool
    Hackle :   Palmered light red cock, ribbed 5 turns oval gold tinsel

4.   *Hook* :   2 down-eyed
    Tip :   Flat gold tinsel
    Body :   Peacock herl
    Hackle :   Palmered Greenwell cock, ribbed gold wire

5.   *Hook* :   3 down-eyed
    Body :   Blue dun seal's fur
    Hackle :   Palmered blue dun cock, possibly ribbed 4 turns wire

6.   Grayling Witch
    Hook :   000 down-eyed
    Tag :   Red stained feather fibre
    Body :   Green peacock herl, ribbed flat silver tinsel
    Hackle :   White cock

7. **Bradshaw's Fancy**
    Hook :   00 sneck, down-eyed
    Tag :   Red floss, head and tail
    Body :   Green peacock herl
    Hackle :   Blue dun hen

8. *Hook* :   3 down-eyed
    Tag :   Red floss, head and tail
    Body :   Bronze peacock herl
    Hackle :   Pale blue dun cock, short

Aphids and Midges

1. *Hook* :   000 double, down-eyed
    *(Woolley's original patterns of this sort were dressed on two singles
    bound together with silk. He preferred this method as he considered it
    gave greater flexibility to the fly, avoiding hook breakages through
    leverage when a fish was being played.)*
    Whisks :   Greenwell cock hackle fibres three times length of body
    Body :   Yellow silk, ribbed 3 turns oval gold tinsel
    Hackle :   Greenwell cock
    Wing :   Starling

2. *Hook* :   Smaller than 000, down-eyed
    Body :   Yellow or pale olive silk
    Hackle :   Bushy, badger cock

3. **G R H E**
    Hook :   Smaller than 000, down-eyed
    Whisks :   Red cock
    Body :   Hare's ear fur, ribbed 2 turns flat gold tinsel
    Hackle :   Light red cock
    Wing :   Upright starling

4. *Hook* :   Smaller than 000, up-eyed
    Body :   Rotund, light orange wool or dubbing
    Hackle :   Blue dun cock

Duns and Dry Flies

1. *Hook* :   000 up-eyed
    Body :   Orange silk
    Hackle :   Bushy, black cock
    Wing :   Possibly corncrake feather fibre or cinnamon hen

2. *Hook* :   000 sneck, up-eyed
    Whisks :   Blue dun cock hackle fibres
    Body :   Grey dubbing - probably rabbit under-fur – ribbed 4 turns gold
                   wire

3. *Hook* :   00 down-eyed
    Body :   Hare's ear dubbing, ribbed 4 turns gold wire
    Hackle :   Red cock
    Wing :   Dark starling or blackbird

4. *Hook* :   00 - 3 sneck, down-eyed
    Whisks :   Long, blue dun cock
    Body :   Grey rabbit under-fur
    Hackle :   Blue dun cock
    Wing :   Light starling

5. *Hook* :   00 up-eyed
    Body :   Stripped peacock herl
    Hackle :   Light blue dun cock
    Wing :   Upright, starling

6.   *Hook* :   0 down-eyed
      Body :   Orange silk, ribbed 4 turns gold wire
      Hackle :   Bushy, Greenwell cock
      Wing :   Hen blackbird

7.   *Hook* :   0 down-eyed
      Whisks :   Light red hen hackle fibres
      Body :   Pale olive dubbing
      Hackle :   Red cock
      Wing :   Dark starling or blackbird

8.   *Hook* :   000 - 0 down-eyed
      Tip :   Flat gold tinsel
      Whisks :   Long, Greenwell cock hackle fibres
      Body :   Yellow silk, ribbed up to 5 turns gold wire
      Hackle :   Two, intermingled ginger and blue dun cock

9.   *Hook* :   000 up-eyed
      Whisks :   Greenwell cock
      Body :   Olive dyed stripped quill
      Hackle :   White or very pale blue dun
      Wing :   Upright, dun feather fibre

10.   *Hook* :   000 sneck, up-eyed
      Whisks :   Black cock
      Body :   Hare's ear fur dubbed on red silk
      Hackle :   Bushy, dark brown cock
      Wing :   Dark brown feather fibre

11.   *Hook* :   000 up-eyed
      Whisks :   Long, red cock
      Body :   Yellow silk, ribbed 3 turns gold wire
      Hackle :   Dark red cock
      Wing :   Two small buff feathers tied upright and clipped short

12.   *Hook* :   000 down-eyed
     Whisks :   Long, cream or buff cock
     Body :   Stripped peacock quill
     Hackle :   White or pale blue dun cock
     Wing :   Upright, cinnamon-buff feather fibre - possibly corncrake

13.   *Hook* :   000 sneck, up-eyed
     Body :   White silk
     Hackle :   White cock
     Wing :   Upright, white feather fibre

14.   *Hook* :   000 down-eyed
     Whisks :   Blue dun cock hackle fibres
     Body :   Orange silk
     Hackle :   Blue dun cock
     Wing :   Cinnamon feather fibre, possibly corncrake

15.   G R H E
     Hook :   000 down-eyed
     Whisks :   Blue dun cock
     Body :   Hare's ear fur, ribbed 4 turns gold wire
     Hackle :   None
     Wing :   Upright, dark starling

16.   *Hook* :   000 up-eyed
     Whisks :   Golden pheasant tippets
     Body :   Flat gold tinsel
     Hackle :   Red cock
     Wing :   Pale grey feather fibre

17.   *Hook* :   00 up-eyed
     Whisks :   Speckled cock
     Body :   Stripped peacock herl
     Hackle :   Badger cock
     Wing :   Dark brown feather fibre

18.   *Hook* :   00 up-eyed
        Whisks :   Cream cock hackle fibres
        Body :   Pale orange dubbing
        Hackle :   Pale blue dun
        Wing :   Upright, two pairs, starling

19.   *Hook* :   00 up-eyed
        Whisks :   Blue dun cock hackle fibres
        Body :   Stripped peacock herl
        Hackle :   Blue dun cock
        Wing :   Upright, dark starling

20.   *Hook* :   00 up-eyed
        Whisks :   Light red hen hackle fibres
        Body :   Stripped peacock herl
        Hackle :   Light red cock
        Wing :   Upright, two pairs, starling

21.   *Hook* :   00 up-eyed
        Whisks :   Cream cock hackle fibres
        Body :   Stripped peacock herl, dark
        Hackle :   Dun cock
        Wing :   Upright, two pairs, possibly hen blackbird - medium brown

22. **Iron Blue Variant?**
        Hook :   00 up-eyed
        Whisks :   3, fine peacock herl
        Body :   Stripped peacock herl, stained purple
        Hackle :   Red cock
        Wing :   Iron blue feather fibre

23.   *Hook* :   00 down-eyed
        Body :   Light olive seal's fur or wool ribbed 3 turns gold wire
        Hackle :   Long, light blue cock

24. **Sedge**

    Hook :   00 up-eyed
    Body :   Yellow-olive silk, ribbed 4 turns gold wire
    Hackle :   Bushy Greenwell cock
    Wing :   Woodcock wing quill fibre tied flat

25.   *Hook* :   00 down-eyed
    Whisks :   Dark brown cock hackle fibres
    Body :   Sepia dubbing
    Hackle :   Dark brown cock
    Wing :   Dark brown feather fibre, clipped
    Head :   Large, orange silk

26.   *Hook* :   0 sneck, down-eyed
    Tip :   Flat gold tinsel
    Butt :   Green peacock herl
    Body :   Crimson silk
    Thorax :   Green peacock herl
    Hackle :   Bushy, cinnamon cock
    Wing :   Upright, paired, stiff pale grey feather fibre

27.   *Hook* :   0 up-eyed
    Whisks :   Red cock
    Body :   Flat gold tinsel and palmered red cock hackle, ribbed gold wire
    Hackle :   Blue dun, several turns

28. **Wickham's Fancy**

    Hook :   0 up-eyed
    Whisks :   Long, light red cock
    Body :   Flat gold tinsel and palmered red cock hackle, ribbed gold wire
    Wing :   Upright, paired, starling

29. *Hook* : 0 sneck, down-eyed
    Whisks : Light red cock
    Body : Greenish-brown silk
    Hackle : Bushy red cock
    Wing : Starling

30. *Hook* : 0 sneck, down-eyed
    Whisks : Dun feather fibre
    Body : Stripped peacock herl
    Hackle : Blue dun cock
    Wing : Upright, pale starling

31. *Hook* : 0 down-eyed
    Whisks : Buff feather fibre
    Body : Light dun seal's fur
    Hackle : Dun cock

32. *Hook* : 0 down-eyed
    Body : Cream seal's fur, ribbed 4 turns oval gold tinsel
    Hackle : Bushy, long, pale blue dun

33. *Hook* : 0 sneck, up-eyed
    Tip : Red-brown stripped quill
    Body : Claret silk, ribbed 5 turns of quill.
    (The body appears to have been varnished).
    Hackle : Medium red cock
    Wing : Pale starling

34. Coachman
    Hook : 0 down-eyed
    Body : Bronze peacock herl
    Hackle : Red cock
    Wing : White feather fibre

35. Alder
   Hook :   1 sneck, down-eyed
   Tip :   Flat gold tinsel
   Body :   Green peacock herl
   Hackle :   Black cock
   Wing :   Tied flat over back:
            1. Dark woodcock wing quill fibre.
            2. Mottled dun feather fibre

36. *Hook* :   1 sneck, down-eyed
   Whisks :   Long, red cock hackle fibres
   Body :   Green peacock herl
   Hackle :   Dun cock
   Wing :   Upright, starling

37. *Hook* :   3 up-eyed
   Whisks :   Red cock hackle fibres
   Body :   Cock pheasant tail fibres, ribbed 4 turns
   Hackle :   Bushy, red cock
   Wing :   Upright grey feather fibre

Wet flies

1. Coch-y-Bondhu Variant
   Hook :   00-0 down-eyed
   Body :   Peacock herl, ribbed 3 turns oval gold tinsel
   Hackle :   Bushy, rich red cock

2. *Hook* :   00 sneck, down-eyed
   Body :   Dun wool
   Hackle :   Magenta stained cock
   Wing :   Bronze mallard

237

3. *Hook* :   00 down-eyed
    Body :   Orange dubbing, ribbed peacock herl
    Hackle :   Black cock
    Wing :   Partridge or hen pheasant wing quill

4. *Hook* :   00 sneck, down-eyed
    Body :   Peacock herl
    Hackle :   Black hen
    Wing :   Brown partridge

5. *Hook* :   0 to gut
    Whisks :   Very long, speckled cock
    Body :   Hare's ear fur, ribbed 3 turns flat gold tinsel
    Hackle :   Speckled brown partridge

6. *Hook* :   0 to gut
    Body :   Hare's ear fur, ribbed 4 turns flat gold tinsel
    Hackle :   Speckled brown partridge
    Wing :   Grouse

7. *Hook* :   0 down-eyed
    Whisks :   Long, black cock
    Body :   Purple silk, ribbed 4 turns oval gold tinsel
    Hackle :   Sparse, black cock
    Wing :   Dark, bronze mallard

8. *Hook* :   00 to gut
    Tail :   Red ibis
    Body :   Black seal's fur, ribbed 4 turns flat gold tinsel
    Hackle :   Black hen
    Wing :   Starling dressed wet

9. *Hook* :   1 down-eyed, long shank
    Tail :   Red floss silk
    Body :   Flat silver tinsel with a light blue dun hen hackle half way down

Hackle : Light blue dun hen

Wing : Pale starling

(This pattern is dressed in a similar style to a worm fly).

10. *Hook* : 1 down-eyed

    Whisks : Ginger cock hackle fibres

    Body : Blue dun seal's fur

    Hackle : Blue dun cock

    Wing : Starling tied wet

11. *Hook* : 1 down-eyed

    Whisks : Magenta stained cock

    Body : Turquoise seal's fur, ribbed 4 turns oval gold tinsel

    Hackle : Dun hen

    Wing : Speckled dun feather fibre

12. **Woodcock and Green**

    Hook : 1 to gut

    Whisks : Long, golden pheasant tippet

    Body : Light olive seal's fur mixed with hare's ear fur, ribbed 4 turns oval gold tinsel

    Hackle : Brown speckled partridge

    Wing : Woodcock wing quill fibre

    Whisks : Golden pheasant tippets

    Body : Fiery brown seal's fur, darker section at the tail end

    Hackle : Dark red hen

    Wing : Cinnamon hen tied wet

13. **Butcher Variant**

    Hook : 1 to gut

    Tail : Orange feather fibre - possibly faded red ibis

    Body : Flat silver tinsel

    Hackle : Black hen

    Wing : Crow

14. **Dunkeld**

Hook :	2 to gut
Whisks :	Blue dun cock hackle fibres
Body :	Flat gold tinsel
Hackle :	Orange stained cock
Wing :	Blue mallard wing quill fibre

15.

Hook :	2 to gut
Whisks :	3 Golden pheasant tippets
Body :	Cream, crimson and purple dubbing in even thirds, ribbed 4 turns gold oval tinsel
Hackle :	Black cock
Wing :	Woodcock, possibly grouse wing quill fibre tied wet

16. **March Brown**

Hook :	2 down-eyed
Whisks :	Speckled brown feather fibres
Body :	Hare's ear fur, ribbed 3 turns flat gold tinsel
Hackle :	Speckled brown partridge
Wing :	Brown partridge wing quill fibre

17. **Grouse and Claret Variant**

Hook :	2 to gut
Whisks :	Golden pheasant topping
Tip :	Flat gold tinsel
Body :	Claret seal's fur, ribbed 4 turns oval gold tinsel
Hackle :	Stained red cock
Wing :	Grouse feather fibre

18.

Hook :	3 to gut
Whisks :	Golden pheasant tippets
Body :	Red seal's fur, ribbed 5 turns oval gold tinsel
Hackle :	Bushy black cock

19. *Hook* :   3 to gut, sneck
    Body :   Flat copper tinsel
    Hackle :   Black cock
    Wing :   Woodcock wing quill

20. *Hook* :   3 to gut, japanned
    Tip :   Flat gold tinsel
    Whisks :   Red cock hackle fibres
    Body :   Peacock herl rubbed off or dark feather herl
    Hackle :   Red cock
    Wing :   Pale starling

21. *Hook* :   4 sneck, down-eyed
    Whisks :   Brown feather fibre
    Body :   Stripped peacock herl
    Hackle :   Dun hen
    Wing :   Starling

22. *Hook* :   5 sneck, down-eyed
    Body :   Pale brown silk, ribbed 5 turns round gold tinsel
    Hackle :   Red cock
    Wing :   Starling tied long

23. *Hook* :   5 down-eyed
    Body :   Fine oval gold tinsel, ribbed 4 turns thicker oval silver tinsel
    Hackle :   Two, red cock and sooty black cock
    Wing :   Grey feather fibre

24. Alexandra
    Hook :   6 to gut, japanned
    Tail :   3 green peacock swords
    Body :   Flat silver tinsel
    Hackle :   Black cock
    Wing :   Green peacock swords with red ibis over
    Cheeks :   Jungle cock

A further set of flies, in the possession of a relative of Roger Woolley, contains three patterns which may be of interest to anglers in the Welsh Borders and North Shropshire. They are labelled *Tanat Steel Blue*, *Tanat Cinnamon* and *Tanat Green Insect* in handwriting similar to that of Roger Woolley and are contained in a Woolley hook packet with an unusual transparent, overprinted, cellophane cover. This was certainly printed before the foundation of the limited company. The names of these patterns may be familiar in the localities of the River Tanat but my research has failed to find them. If they are Roger's original patterns it may be that the flies were dressed at the request of local clients or for Roger's own use on visits as he had connections in the area. He certainly appeared to name some of his original patterns with a prefix or other description which defined the waters on which he or others used them – the 'Costa' series and 'The Brailsford' being other examples. How they were named can now only be subject to speculation, but it does seem quite a coincidence that perhaps Roger's favourite pattern, the Steel Blue, should appear in a variant form as the Tanat Steel Blue.

1. **Tanat Steel Blue**

   Hook : 1, sneck, down-eyed

   Butt : Two or three turns of orange silk

   Body : Dark green peacock herl, bushy. No obvious ribbing but wire may be hidden in the herl

   Hackle : Palmered black or very dark blue dun cock, quite long in the fibre

   (Unlike the Grayling Steel Blue the head is black.)

2. **Tanat Cinnamon**

   Hook : 1, sneck, down-eyed

   Body : Brown feather fibre with short flue wound tight and dressed short, ribbed 5 turns gold wire

   Hackle : Cinnamon cock, long in the fibre, several turns. Some fibres lie back under the body and extend beyond the hook bend

3.   Tanat Green Insect

   Hook :   1, sneck, down-eyed
   Tag :   Red floss silk, extending beyond hook bend
   Body :   Bright green peacock herl, wound tight and close, possibly
             ribbed with tight turns silver wire
   Hackle : Badger cock, quite long and bushy

Tanat flies in cellophane hook packet

243

Index

A SELECTION OF KEY BOOKS
ON THE HISTORY AND PRACTICE OF FLY-TYING
AVAILABLE FROM COCH-Y-BONDDU BOOKS

A HISTORY OF FLYFISHING   Conrad Voss Bark

THE DRY FLY: PROGRESS SINCE HALFORD   Conrad Voss Bark

JIM WYNN'S RECOMMENDED FLIES FOR THE RIVER WHARFE   Martin Cross

BROOK & RIVER TROUTING   HH Edmonds & NN Lee

PLU STINIOG: TROUT FLIES FOR NORTH WALES   Emrys Evans

THE ESSENTIAL KELSON: A FLY-TYER'S COMPENDIUM   Terry Griffiths

FLY-FISHING IN IRELAND   Tommy Hanna

FM HALFORD & THE DRY FLY REVOLUTION   Tony Hayter

ANGLING GIANTS: ANGLERS WHO MADE HISTORY   Andrew Herd

THE FLY: A NEW HISTORY OF FLYFISHING   Andrew Herd

ORANGE OTTER   Christopher Knowles

NYMPH FISHING: A HISTORY   Terry Lawton

FLYFISHING: THE NORTH COUNTRY TRADITION   Leslie Magee

IRISH TROUT & SALMON FLIES   EJ Malone

TYING FLIES IN THE IRISH STYLE   EJ Malone

A MAN MAY FISH   TC Kingsmill Moore

FRENCH FISHING FLIES   Jean-Paul Pequegnot

NORTH COUNTRY FLIES   TE Pritt

THE FLY-FISHER'S ENTOMOLOGY   Alfred Ronalds

FLYFISHING THE WELSH BORDERLANDS: A REVIEW OF FLYFISHING
    & FLIES FOR WILD TROUT AND GRAYLING   Roger Smith

THE PRACTICAL ANGLER   WC Stewart

LIST OF WHARFEDALE FLIES   John Swarbrick

ANGLING WITH THE FLY: FLIES & ANGLERS OF DERBYSHIRE
    & STAFFORDSHIRE   JN Watson

HALFORD – SKUES – PRITT – MOTTRAM – FRANCIS – SAWYER – KITE –
DUNNE – OVERFIELD – VENIARD – BLACKER – GORDON – HILLS

ALL of the important books on flyfishing and fly-tying are in stock, usually both
in their original editions and as modern facsimiles in the *Flyfisher's Classic Library*
series. If you cannot see the book you require on our website, please ask. Paul will find
you a copy.

COCH-Y-BONDDU BOOKS   www.anglebooks.com   01654-702837

If you have enjoyed
The Forgotten Flies of Roger Woolley
may we suggest *Angling with the Fly*
also by J N Watson

Angling with the Fly: Flies and Anglers of Derbyshire & Staffordshire charts the history and development of flyfishing in these two counties. John Watson's detailed research brings together, for the first time, the lives and backgrounds of many notable flyfishers. He discusses, in depth, the evolution of local fly patterns from the 18th and 19th centuries up to the present day. The book is very well illustrated throughout with plates of flies from Aldam, Foster, Roger Woolley and other early writers and fly-tyers, and with many double-page spreads of the flies of more recent Derbyshire flyfishers. Many of the traditional flies have been tied by Tim Thorpe and photographed by Terry Griffiths.

There are excellent historical sections on angling luminaries including Charles Cotton, W.H. Aldam, Alfred Ronalds, John Turton, William Shipley and David Foster, with lists of their fly-patterns, as well as Izaak Walton, T.C. Hofland, John Beever, James Ogden, the Marquess of Granby, William H. Foster, Edward Marston, Walter M. Gallichan, Gerald G.P. Heywood, Wilfred Louis Foster, A. Nelson Bromley, Roger Woolley, and present-day authorities: John Neville, Tony Bridgett, Steve Trigg, Steve Woolley, Tim Thorpe and Peter Arfield. A must-have reference work for the angling historian.

COCH-Y-BONDDU BOOKS

WWW.ANGLEBOOKS.COM

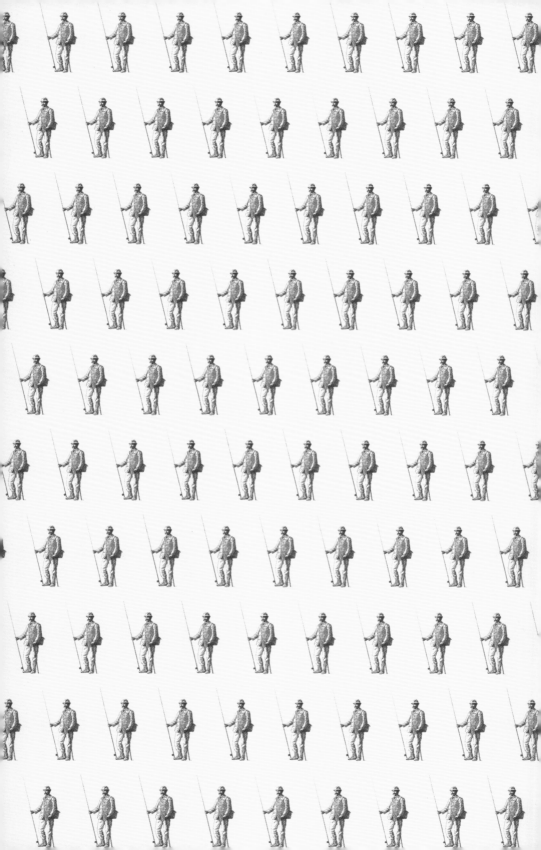